With equal measures of honesty
story of how God wooed her thr

—**Jonathan Rogers**, author and host of The Habit Membership for Writers

Kori Morgan's *Why I Dyed My Hair Purple and Other Unorthodox Stories* inhabits the wondrous journey where self-discovery and God-discovery meet. Her captivating tales exhibit the little-known serendipity wherein human tenacity in *conscientious* self-determination and God's tenacious pursuit of us converge. Seeing Kori's encounters with the *common characters* of life we all face—whether bad or good—and the *common graces* available through cultural icons like Buddy Holly, Johnny Cash, U2, and the Indigo Girls, is edge-of-your-seat drama sure to embolden all readers toward their own God-given life-discovery.

—**Bryan M. Christman**, author of *The Gospel in the Dock* and the book series *A Kierkegaardian Reading of the Gospel of Mark*

Kori Morgan's essays are a meeting place, a bridge between those on the fringes and those who struggle to understand their friends on the fringes. Nuanced and beautiful, honest and orthodox, her essays invite readers in, telling her story in such a way that it points through itself to the sunlight outside.

—**Théa Rosenburg**, co-editor of *Wild Things and Castles in the Sky* and founder of *Little Book, Big Story*

At a moment when our culture seems to see art and religion as diametrically opposed, and when artists within the church at large seem invisible—unless they can offer it tangible, quantifiable gifts—Morgan's experience, biblical knowledge and interpretation shines a light for those of us who feel torn between the gifts we have been given, and our faith. What I appreciated about Morgan's perspective is that she gives me hope—hope that I can love my church, my art and God, and not feel like a "failure." I also appreciate that this book is a work of art. Morgan writes with elegance and clarity, humor and passion. And while she acknowledges that manmade stories have limitations, they are often the crucial domino that needs to be poked in order for our false conceptions of truth to collapse one by one. I believe these stories will be the crucial domino for many readers.

—**Charity Gingerich**, author of *After June* (Green Writers Press)

WHY I DYED MY HAIR

PURPLE

AND OTHER

UNORTHODOX STORIES

KORI MORGAN

CALLA PRESS
PUBLISHING

Published by Calla Press Publishing
Texas Countryside
United States 76401

Cover Design: Founder of Calla Press Publishing
First Printing, 2025
Printed in the USA

Unless otherwise indicated, Scripture quotations are from the ESV Bible (The Holy Bible, English Standard Version), copyright @ 2001 by Crossway, a publishing ministry of Good News Publishers.

All emphases in Scripture quotations have been added by the author.

Some names and identifiable features have been changed to protect the privacy of the individuals.

Trade paperback ISBN: 979-8-9888702-4-1

To my husband, Curtis, for bearing witness to my story, and to Leslie Bustard—until we meet again in the city of blinding lights.

CONTENTS

1. So Teach Us to Number Our Days 9
2. Messengers 11
3. Her Nose Stuck In A Book 14
4. The Only 18
5. Buddy 22
6. Why I Didn't Believe in God 25
7. The Dwarf at the Stone Table 29
8. The Liturgy of Borders 32
9. Midnight in Missoula 34
10. Why The Shawshank Redemption is My Favorite Movie 37
11. This is my Body 39
12. Closer to Fine 42
13. Verily, Verily, I Say Unto Thee 46
14. God's Gonna Cut You Down 50
15. Owl Walk 54
16. Wise Blood 56
17. I Didn't Become a Christian Because of My Near-Death Experience 61
18. The Woman with the Issue of Blood 64
19. See, Here is Water 69
20. A Lesson from Javert 74
21. She Will Be Saved Through Childbearing 81
22. Why I Dyed My Hair Purple 84
23. At Least There Were Bluebirds 89
24. Miracle Drug 92
25. Did You Know Jesus Can Breathe Underwater? 96
26. Near Misses 98
27. Sunlight 100
28. The Virtuous Woman 103
29. The Fellowship of Kindred Minds 108
Acknowledgments 117
About the Author 121

SO TEACH US TO NUMBER OUR DAYS

The mural stretched over the grand oak doors that led into the school auditorium. Painted against a beige-brown, scroll-like background, its medieval-style script spelled out Psalm 90:12 in maroon letters: "*So teach us to number our days, that we may apply our hearts unto wisdom.*"[1] It was a gift from the class of 1925, back when the spacious building was brand-new and housed the high school students. By the time I was a student there in the late '90s, it had been repurposed as the district's middle school. The mural was still there, deemed a historical artifact by the Board of Education.

The summer before I started seventh grade, middle school loomed like an oncoming storm. I couldn't stop thinking about the multiple classes I'd have to navigate in the old building's labyrinth of corridors, the locker combination I was sure to lose, and the sixth-grade bullies picking up where they'd left off the year before.

But that wasn't how it turned out. On the first day of school, a new group of friends invited me to sit with them at lunch. I loved my teachers and the new and varied structure of my day. I quickly memorized my locker combination.

---

1 Ps. 90:12 KJV

Later, I found my niche in the school's wide array of activities. I made fourth-chair violin in the school orchestra. One of my new friends encouraged me to try out for drama club, and I landed a lead role in the fall play. I found myself practically living in the old auditorium for music and play rehearsals, occupying a corner seat in the front row where I studied my lines and did homework.

And every time I walked through those big oak doors, I saw that mural.

So teach us to number our days.

I didn't know what that meant. Was it like counting the days until vacation? Like in that *Amelia Bedelia* book where she's told to add dates to a cake but puts in cut-up pieces from a calendar instead?

I knew the phrase was from the Bible. I wasn't sure if God was real, but I still wondered what it meant, as if it were a secret message left behind by those long-ago students for me to decode.

Years later, after I became a Christian, I came across the verse during a Bible study. I was instantly taken back to that doorway and everything beyond it—the anticipation of opening night, the excitement of a music rehearsal, my fingers itching to play the violin. The feeling of belonging that replaced my initial fear and insecurity about entering a new school and a new chapter of life.

I don't know how God was with me then or what he tried to teach me through that century-old mural. But I know this: the God I did not believe in saw me, a teenager with long hair, green-painted nails, and a blue backpack slung over my shoulder. On that stage, he gave me music, plays, and stories that delighted me, knowing I would someday see the full extent of what God has prepared for those who love him.[2]

I think of the mural whenever I read Psalm 90, imagining the students in long skirts and dapper ties selecting it as their class gift so many years ago. I picture them praying over its commission, unaware that someday, it would be buried like a seed in a thirteen-year-old girl's memory until she was ready to receive its growth.

---

2 1 Cor. 2:9 ESV

MESSENGERS

Early in my life, my parents decided they would not take me to church. My mother grew up in an Italian Roman Catholic family and went to a school with nuns who smacked her knuckles with a ruler for disobeying in class. My dad's mother called herself a Christian but only acted like one at church; at home, she wielded Bible verses like weapons, demanding that her children honor their mother even as she berated and beat them.

As a result, my parents decided they would raise me without any religion. When I was ready, I could make that choice on my own.

After my dad's mother found out I wasn't going to church, she harshly rebuked him. He would someday have to give an account for leading his family astray. My dad told her she had interesting thoughts on raising children considering how she'd treated her own family.

My parents and I never said it out loud, but none of us liked going to visit Grandma. Her hugs were suffocating and she smelled like oppressive floral deodorant. She had a special gift for burning food, so going to her house always meant charred meat, carbonized vegetables, and canned prayers before meals that reeked of insincere piety. *Come, Lord Jesus, be our guest. Let these gifts to us be blessed*, she recited. Across the table, my dad cringed.

One afternoon around Christmas, my dad had a dentist appointment that he suspected would take a while. Since my grandmother lived three blocks from the office, he opted to leave me at her house rather than take me along. I assumed the afternoon would mean listening to her pound out hymns on the piano and pretending to eat indigestible food.

But when I walked in, the kitchen smelled fresh and sugary. The table was covered with a white plastic tablecloth and little bowls of icing, sprinkles, and tiny, decorative balls of sugar. It looked like the cover of a Martha Stewart book on how to make precious holiday memories with your kids. Grandma announced that we would be decorating Christmas cookies for the afternoon.

She turned on the radio, which was playing holiday music for the grand ramp-up to Christmas. The cookies were angel-shaped, with long dresses and broad wings. With Bing Crosby humming in the background, I took a plastic spoon and began icing my angel, forming her a halo with little balls of sugar. Grandma explained that the angels were God's messengers who told the wise men and shepherds about the baby Jesus.

I kept decorating my cookie, only half-listening to the story. I got too much icing on my fingers and licked it off. As I was sucking the sugary goodness off my fingers, Grandma leaned forward on one elbow and told me that my parents didn't believe in Jesus and that they didn't want me to believe in him either. That meant we were all going to hell.

I messed up the icing on my cookie. My forehead crinkled up, and I felt sick to my stomach. I hadn't realized how rich the icing was, and I wondered if maybe I ate too much of it. I considered asking Grandma what hell was and what I'd done to be sent there, but the question carried so much weight that I felt as if my mind would collapse underneath it. I pushed the thoughts away, finished decorating the cookie, and then asked if I could eat one without icing.

When my dad came to pick me up, Grandma sent me out the door with a Ziploc bag full of cookies. I climbed into the passenger seat of my dad's van and tossed the bag over my shoulder into the backseat. Dad asked if I had a good time with Grandma; I asked him if I was going to hell.

He froze and blinked. He was silent for a moment, and gradually, a cold look of recognition fell over his face. His jaw stiffened. "Wait here," he ordered. Then he got out of the car, slammed the door, and went back into Grandma's house.

He was in there for a long time. I wondered what he was saying to her and why he was so angry. Eventually, he came back outside muttering under his breath, his brow furrowed, and we drove home. In the silence, I wondered what kind of God would send my family to hell when we hadn't even done anything wrong. But I didn't really want an answer. I was just glad that my parents didn't make me go to church or do anything that would force me to confront a God who was angry at me and apparently didn't care if I knew why.

I didn't know there was more to the story.

HER NOSE STUCK IN A BOOK

When I was in first grade, my teacher called my mom and dad in for a conference. I imagined they were a little concerned, considering I had a "discipline problem" in kindergarten. I wasn't particularly wild or disobedient—I was just strange. I'd take books in the bathroom and read during class because I was bored with the lessons about the alphabet. I played with plastic dinosaurs that I brought to school and sat in the corner alone acting out stories with them. I never followed instructions for daily projects; I'd draw a picture of my imaginary friends when I was supposed to be drawing my favorite family member or design my own popsicle stick house instead of following the prescribed blueprint.

At the meeting, my parents and my teacher sat around his desk in our classroom, surrounded by our construction paper collages and the puppets he used in his lessons. He explained that I was a great student, a strong reader, always ready to help my classmates . . . but I didn't play with the other kids during recess. Instead, I wandered around in a bit of a daze, talking to myself and intently gesturing at the world around me, seemingly oblivious to all the other children. Sometimes I'd sit in the corner of the playground, ignoring everyone until the bell rang and it was time to go back to class.

Here we go again, I imagine my mom thought.

Later that night, she casually asked me about what I liked to do at recess and if I played any nice games with my friends. I quickly became irate and said that because I was now at school all day instead of just a half-day like in kindergarten, recess was the only time I had to tell stories and read.

Our playground was a wonderland: a vast expanse of swings, metal slides, monkey bars, and a red, steel-framed fire truck with a wooden floor and a plastic steering wheel. Beyond the swings and slides, though, there were places that struck me as even more wondrous. An alcove in the far corner near the back of the fire truck was draped with low-hanging branches, a concrete barrier holding up the rusted chain-link fence surrounding it. In my mind, it became a secret cave, an imaginary kingdom where my secret adventures could unfold. How could playing games with the other students compare to that?

Once my teacher understood what I was doing during recess, he encouraged me to write my stories down and would even let me read them to the class. But the rest of the students didn't understand. To them, I was the teacher's pet, the "weird kid," and they teased me for telling stories and reading so much.

It hurt, but it also didn't. Part of me wanted to conform to what I was supposed to be, to join their games of kickball and Red Rover and try to blend in. Life would be easier if I was just like everyone else. But in the end, I didn't know how to do that. The only thing I knew how to do was wander around the playground as I watched my imaginary world take shape, the stories spiraling out in front of me like an unfurled role of party streamers. So, I put up with the teasing, the pointing, and the whispering even as I continued to be a storyteller. No matter how naturally it came to me, though, I still always wondered if I was okay.

On my seventh birthday, my parents took me to see *Beauty and the Beast*. It was the film's opening day, and the theater was so packed that we had to sit way down in the front, the screen practically on top of us. I leaned my head back and watched the opening prologue unfold—the selfish prince transformed into a beast by the enchantress in disguise, all staged in stained-glass pictures. I loved fairy tales, and the minor tones of the score slowly wrapped around me like a cloak, drawing me in as it set the stage for the plot to come.

And then Belle stepped onto the screen. As she meandered down the hill into town from her small house, I was instantly drawn to her. She had brown hair like mine, but more importantly, she carried a book. I watched her wander through town, reading as she sang about feeling trapped in a simple place with simple-minded people, while all around her, the villagers gossiped about how strange she was and how she didn't fit in. Still, she continued to walk with the book open in her hands, engrossed in the story, pushing their words away.

On the enormous screen, the scene overtook every inch of my vision. I felt a kind of comfort well up inside me that I'd never experienced before. I started to cry. In the dark, my mom leaned over and asked if I was okay. I said yes. I was so happy because Belle was just like me.

I knew immediately that I really was okay no matter what the other kids thought. I knew I could return to school the next week with renewed confidence. If Belle could remain steadfast under the pressure to conform, so could I.

Author Mitali Perkins, who immigrated to the United States with her Bengali family when she was young, has written extensively about how books transformed her life as a child living in a strange country. "Books were my rock, my stability, my safe place as I navigated the border between California suburbia and the Bengali culture of my traditional home," she explains in her author biography.[1] In a similar way, it was a Disney movie that allowed me to gain confidence in being different. Belle showed me that it was okay to celebrate my creative spirit even if other people didn't understand.

It was the renewal and reassurance I desperately needed, and it came through the medium I loved the most: a story.

---

1 Perkins, Mitali. "About Me." Mitali Perkins, accessed June 6, 2024. https://www.mitaliperkins.com/p/about-me.html.

As an adult, I still draw strength from fictional characters to whom I relate. However, after I became a Christian later in life, I discovered that there is something greater than the kinship I felt with my favorite characters. I am a new creation in Jesus Christ. I am his workmanship, created for the good works the Father has prepared for me.[2] Often, these works involve telling stories of my own, although people often question them, saying they are too religious, or by contrast, not religious enough.

Despite the pressures I continue to face, my objective is not to conform, but to obey in the work I've been given, because being myself is still the only thing I know how to do.

---

2   Eph. 2:10 ESV

THE ONLY

I don't know what it's like to have siblings. My parents had me late in life. They went through complications with me, but they still wanted to try for another child. I remember my mom doing things I didn't understand at the time, like taking her temperature every morning and charting the numbers in a notebook.

She asked me once if I would like to have a brother or sister. I don't remember my answer, but no baby ever came. For the rest of my life, I would remain the only one.

It never occurred to me that there was anything unusual about being an only child, not even when I went over to my friends' houses to play. My best friend had a younger brother who always joined in our activities. The three of us formed a secret club together, and in my eyes, he was more my friend than he was her sibling. The family next door had two sons, and we'd spend the weekends riding bikes and drawing on our driveways with chalk.

At school, we'd draw family portraits. Even when the teacher hung them on the bulletin board and I looked at all the pictures at once, it never struck me as odd that I'd drawn our family dog in the place where everyone else had at least one brother or sister.

The first time I realized there was something different about my family was when I read *Little Women*. I was nine, and the adventures of the March sisters captured my imagination, especially those of Jo and Beth, the family's respective writer and musician. The plays they put on in their attic and the scripts Jo wrote with her sisters made me think of the games and stories my friends and I created together.

But as the story unfolded, I realized that there was a distinct difference. The Marches were a family with four daughters—four sisters. In my family, there was only me.

One night, my mom found me sitting on the floor looking at my Madame Alexander *Little Women* dolls, the four of them lined up against the wall in satin dresses with their sad, staring eyes looking back at me. I felt empty inside, keenly aware that something was missing. My mom approached and asked me if I wished that I had sisters too. I felt my eyes well up with tears.

Although I was lonely sometimes, I was never discontented with being the only one. Still, I knew that it was unusual. I became aware of how people reacted when I said I had no siblings and the unfortunate looks they would give me. I knew that most people would always see my family more for what I lacked than for all I had.

I became a Christian in my early twenties, and soon after that, I met my husband. Not long after we got married, we joined a church plant headed up by the pastor from the church where we'd met. At one of our group's initial meetings, our pastor said we needed families for the church to grow, as well as to produce more soldiers for the Kingdom of God. Before long, we were attracting couples about to have their first or second babies and others who already had anywhere from three to six children. Our pastor once said with a grin that he hoped my husband and I would have at least twelve. I told myself he was just kidding.

One day, I arrived early for the mid-week service and helped him and the Sunday school teacher set up. As I put out Bibles on the folding chairs, he made a casual remark that there was something wrong with me for being an only child. He also implied that, by extension, there was something wrong with me as a Christian.

I had not been raised in a Christian home and wasn't saved until later in life, so I didn't know how this was possible. I don't remember the words he used or how he rationalized it. But I poignantly recall the dismay, the confusion, and finally, the sting. He was saying my faith was corrupted because of something that was out of my—and even my parents'—control.

The tinge of sadness I'd always felt at the absence of a brother or sister hardened into shame. I never imagined that something about my family background could be displeasing to the Lord when none of us had control over how it unfolded.

Several months later, I was in the car with my dad running errands. I can't remember what the original subject of our conversation was, but out of nowhere, one phrase jolted me: *"when your mother had her miscarriage."*

I stopped him right there. I didn't know what he was talking about.

He said it happened around a year before I was born. The pregnancy was a surprise, but they quickly became excited and had already started buying toys and clothes by the time the baby died. The second time they got pregnant, I arrived after a high-risk C-section.

I asked my dad why I was just now learning about this. He told me that my mom probably didn't want to talk about it. "It was bad," he said.

I remembered my mom's notebook with the temperature readings. I had seen my friends deal with the loss of children in the womb, and it hurt to imagine my mom facing that same grief. But I was also intrigued by another thought that came to me, one that shattered how I'd always perceived my family, especially since my pastor's harsh remarks.

I wasn't the only one.

I have a brother or sister who is right now with the Lord. And someday, we will get to meet.

I think about this often, but I also imagine sometimes that the child my parents lost had lived. In my mind, the baby is a girl—my big sister. Her name is Ruth, like our maternal grandmother we never got to meet. Ironically, I'm the one who looks like our grandmother, tall and full-figured, but in my mind, Ruth looks like my mom with her rounded face and small stature.

Ruth is athletic. She is good at math and science and sports. I am good at none of these things, but she tells me to cut myself some slack because she can't write and doesn't like to read, and her stage fright is so bad that she could never give a speech or be in a play. I call her a jock. She calls me a nerd. We laugh about this.

The next time my pastor or someone at church commented about my only-childness, I thought of my sibling and the day we will see each other. I think he or she has known about me for years. Perhaps they are eagerly anticipating that day as much as I am.

I don't know how my life would have been different if Ruth or another brother or sister had been in my life. Family dynamics shape us so much that perhaps I wouldn't even be the same person. It's a reminder of God's sovereignty in strategically placing people in our lives, cultivating a delicate balance between those who dwell together.

The absence or presence of individuals in our lives is carefully ordained as he prepares the spaces between people, knowing they will help us grow into who he has designed us to become.

BUDDY

When I was eleven, I discovered Buddy Holly, the rock and roll pioneer from the 1950s with the nerdy glasses and goofy smile. I was riding in my mom's Honda Civic to some school or family thing when the song "Everyday" came on the oldies station. Its music-box-like arrangement and innocent, lilting vocals captivated me, carrying me to a small, simple world where music had never taken me. Because my dad was a musician, I'd grown up knowing all the words to songs by Crosby, Stills & Nash, Joni Mitchell, David Bowie, and The Mamas & the Papas. I spent hours listening to music with him when I was little and seemed to know the entire Beatles catalog by osmosis.

But this was different. This song was softer, without the anger and jagged notes that marked the artists of the '60s. I loved my dad's music, but I'd never heard anything that sounded quite this real.

Buddy Holly was special because he was the first musician I discovered on my own. The oldies station broadcasted out of Cleveland just blocks from the Rock & Roll Hall of Fame, and they loved music trivia, so I knew more about him than just the names of some songs. I learned that he was one of the first musicians to be inducted, along with talents like Chuck Berry, The Everly Brothers, and, of course, Elvis. These artists were his contemporaries, and together, they'd built rock music as a genre.

But Buddy grabbed my interest in a way that none of them had. Whenever the station played "Everyday," "That'll Be the Day," or "Peggy Sue," my ears perked up just a little more. His tenor voice was youthful and energetic, and he seemed like someone who would be nice to have as a friend. I was quiet and was bullied at my elementary school. Friends were hard for me to find.

I had a cassette tape of Buddy's greatest hits, which I played over and over again, taken by the unique landscape of each of his songs. There was no prescribed formula for his music—his style was at once loud and alive yet also quiet and contemplative. He blasted through the driving guitar riffs of "Rave On," then played with a quiet strum and lowered voice just one track later on "Well All Right." He was his own genre, blending country, R&B, and pop into a style that made any strict categorization impossible. While listening to the radio one day, I discovered, to my horror, that he'd died in a plane crash at age twenty-two. As a child, this seemed old to me, but I somehow knew it was also much too young for someone to die.

I was in love with Buddy. Not in the same way a twelve-year-old is normally in love with a singer—not like my friends who had crushes on Hanson and the Backstreet Boys. It was more serious than that. The way his songs made me feel protected and understood made him less like a rock hero and more like a cool older brother. When I started sixth grade, I printed out a picture of Buddy from our Encarta CD-ROM encyclopedia and hung it in my locker. Until then, I'd always kept my favorite things hidden away; after getting so many threats from bullies, I had learned to keep my head down. If I wasn't careful, people would steal my treasures and break them. But one day, after some kids broke into my locker and defaced Buddy's picture as a joke, I simply printed out another one to hang in its place. After all, that's probably what he would have done.

Buddy made me fearless because he was fearless. In a music industry full of polished crooners and rugged rebels, he had every reason to be insecure. Yet, he was cool without even trying to be—a skinny guy with a Texas accent and glasses who made those things his trademark rather than trying to reform himself and smooth his rough edges.

It was this honesty that made his music travel through time to a lonely kid who felt she had nothing to offer. His lyrics aren't anything profound—it's the earworm melodies that play out in the layering of his effortless solos and rhythm guitar that make his songs great, not their treatises about young love. But nevertheless, even at their most melancholy, his songs brim with hope—that love will overcome loss, that moments of overwhelming joy will be lasting, and that our deepest longings will be fulfilled.

It would still be ten years before I realized that there is only one true source of hope. But in the frequent friendlessness and solitude of those days, Buddy Holly made it something I could touch.

When I was thirteen, we visited some friends in Texas who took me to see his grave. At the cemetery, we followed markers directing us to the grave site. The flat headstone, engraved with music notes, was covered in guitar picks left as offerings from fans. I sat on the ground next to the grave and played my friend's guitar, picking out the three-chord pattern of "Peggy Sue." I'd just started lessons, and it was the only song I knew, even though "Everyday" was my favorite. The notes scattered into the West Texas heat and wind. After I finished playing, I sat there, silent, tracing his name with my eyes.

I didn't know what to say to Buddy. I still don't.

WHY I DIDN'T BELIEVE IN GOD

Amonth after I turned thirteen, my dad almost died. He had surgery to remove his thyroid after a tumor the size of a grapefruit, silently growing throughout his adult life, finally consumed it. Halfway through the operation, his blood pressure plummeted, the doctors had to pack his body in ice, and when he woke up after the surgery, they had no idea why he was alive, if not brain dead.

In the days after the operation, my mom's face stayed in a perpetual flatline. Whenever the phone rang, she would pick up the cordless extension and disappear into another room. Once, we went to visit my dad in the hospital, but since I was underage, I wasn't allowed to go into the ICU. Instead, I stood alone in the cold, institutional white hallway outside the entrance of the unit and waited for my mom. Nobody told me what happened, but I pieced it together anyway from snatches of phone calls I overheard and hushed conversations with friends who came over to visit.

About a week after my dad came home, I was awakened in the middle of the night by a blast of classical music from the living room. I crept out of bed and downstairs, peeking around the corner of the landing. My dad lay on the floor, calling breathlessly for me to get my mom. He'd crawled across the room to turn on the stereo so someone would wake up. *I GOT PAIN*, he gasped. I went upstairs and woke up my mom, who made a run for the stairs. When I tried to follow her, she pushed me back into my bedroom.

I dove under the covers and prayed to . . . *something*. I don't know what. For my dad to not die. For the nightmarish uncertainty we'd lived in since his operation to end. A little while later, the red and blue lights of the police car and ambulance in our driveway sprayed purple across my bedroom wall. I buried my head in my pillow.

The paramedics said he'd had a severe panic attack. This happened more frequently in the weeks to come as my dad struggled with the whiplash of being told he should have died and having to live with the weight of that knowledge. For months afterward, he isolated himself in the basement bedroom, enveloped in fear and cut off from the world.

I missed my dad. I thought of the father who let me help in his art studio when I was a kid, who quit playing music professionally because he loved being a parent so much, who would periodically tell my teacher I had some appointment, then pick me up from school and take me to the movies. But everything was different now, and I was furious with whatever force it was—God or Allah or Buddha or that nameless Something I'd prayed to that night— who had the power to make him better and yet refused to do it.

When I think of my dad's illness, I remember the era as much as the events themselves. I came of age in the late '90s, the days of dial-up internet, Surge, Blockbuster Video, and *Titanic*. The good days—at least, that's what they seem when I look back.

One of my favorite albums was *So Much for the Afterglow* by the alternative rock band Everclear. A lot of the music from that period of my life has faded from my daily consciousness, cast into the mental purgatory of "Oh yeah, I remember that." But *So Much for the Afterglow* is one of the few albums from middle school that still speaks to me. When I listen to it, a strange fusion of time takes place. I am thirteen and thirty-nine at once. I see both the confusion of youth and the clarity that comes later.

The album contains several of Everclear's best-known songs, including "I Will Buy You a New Life" and "Normal Like You." But my favorite track has always been one of the album's deep cuts: "Why I Don't Believe in God." The song tells the story of lead singer Art Alexakis's mother, who had a nervous breakdown during his childhood. Through its emotionally graphic lyrics, it captures the loss of innocence that comes with realizing the ground beneath your feet is unstable. It mixes Everclear's energetic guitar riffs and Alexakis's grungy voice with elements of gospel music, including a banjo line. The song begins soft and hymn-like, but gradually builds from the bridge toward the final chorus, becoming louder and more defiant. It sheds all semblance of these traditional qualities and becomes fully an Everclear song.

It also speaks to a time and place when these experiences and beliefs were my own.

When I first heard "Why I Don't Believe in God," the lyrics cut deep. I thought of eight-year-old Alexakis, lost in the confusion and chaos of his mother's diagnosis. The song describes him being awakened from sleep by her sickness, someone showing up at his school to inform him that she'd been hospitalized, and having a well-meaning relative tell him to trust the doctors to take care of her. The lyrics are tinged with anger at the God who failed him and the unspeakable terror that comes from watching a parent become a walking ghost.

I knew and still know that fear. Alexakis captured not just his childhood nightmare but mine, those terrifying words and interrupted sleep.

Today, the song remains my favorite of Everclear's work. Yet, my love for "Why I Don't Believe in God" is now somewhat discordant. Ten years later, I became a Christian. I put my faith in a merciful God, in heaven and hell, in all the things Alexakis and I both blamed for the suffering of our families.

But what I understand now is that we aren't meant to know why God allows us to suffer. The only thing believers know for certain is that amid life in a sinful world, faith means trusting that the Father subjugates our losses and injustices, brings them under his authority, and will only allow the pain to accomplish his good work of conforming us to the image of the Lord Jesus Christ.

This is a hard saying.

With all this in mind, I occasionally still listen to "Why I Don't Believe in God." For me, there is spiritual value in art that shows my pain reflected back at me—especially knowing that God rescued me not just from the fear and uncertainty of that moment but also from sin and death, a rescue that will last forever.

I no longer listen to the song as an angry teenager trying to navigate a turbulent situation. I can both empathize with the lyrics and thank God for redeeming my pain, looking both back and forward at once, holding in tension the agony of that suffering and the peace I now experience.

Songs like this—even songs about atheism—can thus be beautiful. For me, enfolded in the song is the scared, angry girl I once was, whose life was altered when all the stability she knew was blown apart. Yet, it was music where she found solace, where she saw that she was not alone in her grief, a reality she would carry with her until the time she realized there was someone infinitely greater than music alone—*the Father of mercies and God of all comfort.*[1]

---

1   2 Cor. 1:3 NASB 1995

THE DWARF AT THE STONE TABLE

In high school, I got a part in a community theater production of *The Lion, The Witch, and the Wardrobe*. I played the Dwarf, the White Witch's head minion in her quest to rule Narnia. I took great joy in this role, in my shaggy black wig, enormous, pasted-on eyebrows, and hump-backed leather costume. I walked with a heavy, hunched-over gait, my face contorted in maniacal laughter. My teeth were painted yellow and blacked out. For weeks after the production, stains remained on the transparent brackets of my braces.

My favorite scene to perform was the execution of Aslan. In our staging, my role was to rally the wolves and rebel animals (played by children in gray sweat suits and costume ears), energizing them for the death of the Great Lion who lay bound on the Stone Table. I leaped across the stage with abandon, the child-wolves howling in response. When the White Witch at last killed Aslan, we all erupted into cheers, knowing that her reign over Narnia was surely secure. At one rehearsal, the director said I needed to tone it down—my character's enthusiasm for her crusade was too distracting from the main action onstage.

Because I was raised in a non-religious family, my understanding of God was ambiguous at best. I had heard people say that God was love and that he was good, but I couldn't reconcile this with the fact that, according to my grandmother, I was being sent to hell. By the time I was cast in *The Lion, the Witch, and the Wardrobe*, I'd lost any interest in understanding this and decided there was no God at all.

Yet, I was still angry with him for the direction my life had taken. The aftermath of my dad's illness, the torment of cruel girls at school, and my growing struggle with depression and anxiety left me wondering where God was during all of this. Moreover, the world was so filled with rage and sadness that it didn't make sense for him to just stand by and watch when he was powerful enough to do something.

Yet, there was a paradox in my beliefs that I couldn't reconcile—how can you hate someone you don't believe exists?

As it happened, C.S. Lewis, the creator of Narnia and the Christ figure of Aslan, shared this confusion. In *The Problem of Pain*, he wrote about this contradiction, explaining how, despite their claims that God does not exist, atheists nonetheless continue to rage against him. For them, the painful circumstances of their lives and the world at large seem at odds with what they think a good God should look like. They fail to recognize that Jesus Christ has overcome the world,[1] defeating sin and death. Because of this, he takes the inevitable difficulties we face and uses them to serve the good work he is faithful to complete.[2]

Of course, this reality cannot be understood without believing that Jesus himself is God, having willingly become the sacrifice that makes this victory possible. But at the time I led Narnia's evil creatures in their celebration of Aslan's apparent defeat, the illogical nature of my anger at God was far from my mind. I was fully immersed in my role, gnashing my teeth at Aslan and letting out a loud battle cry as the Witch stabbed a dagger through his shorn body.

---

1   John 16:33 NIV
2   Phil. 1:6 ESV

Years later, though, after I'd become a Christian, I studied Lewis's conversion in *Surprised by Joy*. As I read Lewis's testimony, I was comforted by the similarities between our stories. I learned of his own pain—the loss of his mother at a young age, horrific abuse at the hands of boys at boarding school, and the brutal suffering he endured as a soldier in World War I. His story demonstrated that I was not alone in my rage at God. One of the greatest Christian authors who ever lived, who wrote so beautifully about the struggle of unbelief, had traversed the same spiritual ground I had.

More importantly, we had both arrived at the knowledge of a compassionate, loving God who is sovereign over all things. We both came to understand that he will someday judge the world and bring an end to the sin that sickens the world and the hearts of men.

As a result, when I think of my zeal in that scene in *The Lion, the Witch, and the Wardrobe*, I can't help but see the reality of it: my rebellion against God was evident in my performance. Thoroughly entrenched in the White Witch's cause, the Dwarf does terrible things in her name. He aids in the kidnapping of a child. He arrests and tortures Narnians who resist her reign of terror. All of these actions culminate in facilitating murder by leading the Witch's armies to cry out for Aslan's death.

I think of the masses at the foot of the cross, cheering at the mockery and mutilation of the King and crying out, "Crucify him!" as he accepts their humiliation and torment, silent and set on obeying his Father's plan.

And then I think of myself on that stage, leading the actors playing the Witch's followers in our own acts of scorn.

It was just a play. But I was acting out what was truly in my heart.

THE LITURGY OF BORDERS

Every Saturday night, starting two years after he recovered from his surgery, my dad and I would go to Borders Books and Music. I don't know when these trips became a weekly event, only that I was overjoyed that my dad was himself again and we had this new shared language of beauty and creativity.

What I also remember is that Borders was where the stories were—when we walked through its big wooden doors, everything outside dissolved away. All that remained was its beige bookshelves, the scent of freshly brewed espresso, faux leather armchairs, and friendly blue signs directing us to the different sections of the store. To me, the walls upon walls of books were rivaled only by the castle library in *Beauty and the Beast*.

Our visits followed the same pattern of events. Once we arrived, we decided where in the store we'd each explore and in what order so we could meet up if needed. My dad usually went straight for the movie section but eventually ended up in history, where he'd sit in one of the chairs reading a presidential biography or a coffee table book of World War II battles.

My activities on these outings depended on my current fixation. I might make a beeline for the music, where I'd flip through the wooden CD racks for albums by Nanci Griffith, Gillian Welch, and Lucinda Williams, the plastic security holders *click-click-clicking* as I looked at each album. Occasionally, I was drawn to one of the CDs displayed on a panel of featured new releases, where I could put on a pair of headphones and listen to a few tracks.

Mostly, though, I liked getting lost in the literature section. In ninth grade, I was obsessed with Vladimir Nabokov, entranced by his meandering, poetic writing style and stories that always arrived at a surprising and logical conclusion no matter how many digressions they took. Once, we left Borders with Ayn Rand's *The Fountainhead*, one of my dad's favorite novels, which comforted my angst as a creative person who didn't seem to fit neatly into any social category and wasn't willing to try. I underscored this point by carrying Rand's five-hundred-page monolith around school, reading it during breaks in class or at lunch. The copy he bought me, which he signed with a note of encouragement for my writing pursuits, still occupies a place of honor on my bookshelf, its orange spine battered and faded.

Eventually, Dad and I would land at the café in the corner of the store with our selected purchases. A college student who worked there part-time would ask me about what I was reading that week as she prepared our mocha lattes. We sat next to the big window, looking out at the parking lot as I showed my dad what books or music I wanted to get. He always bought them for me every week, knowing that whatever I picked out, I would devour it and study it in the interceding days. He knew my love of stories and desire to create were the best investments to make for a lonely girl who didn't fit in, who needed the hope of many worlds.

We'd take our selections to checkout, where the clerk tucked my books into a white plastic bag emblazoned with the Border's logo in red. *Have a good night*, he'd say. If the employees at checkout recognized us, they'd give the added benediction of *see you next week*, the promise of more goodness to come, and then we'd walk out the door.

MIDNIGHT IN MISSOULA

During my trip to Texas, where I visited Buddy Holly's grave, I discovered the music of Nanci Griffith. A folk music legend who began her career in the late 1970s, Nanci was a master story-teller; her songs traverse landscapes and decades in just three or four minutes before bringing you home again, somehow wiser and more blessed for having journeyed with her. Her voice was delicate yet edged with the rough twang of her native Texas, like a crystal scratched by dirty pebbles and sand. Ironically, Nanci decided that she wanted to be a singer when she was still a small child—after seeing Buddy Holly perform on *Ed Sullivan*. The connection be-tween two of my beloved artists only made me admire her music even more.

I went to my first Nanci Griffith concert three weeks after be-ginning my junior year of high school. Bathed in blue stage lights, she stepped before the audience wearing a periwinkle, tunic-like dress with a white, iridescent scarf draped around her neck. My parents and I had seats in the fifth row, and being so close to my favorite singer felt surreal and intoxicating. More than once, her eyes seemed to lock with mine, and she gave me a thin, mischievous smile and a wink. Before we left the auditorium that night, I bought a gray t-shirt with her name on the front and the cover of her most recent album, *Clock Without Hands*, on the back.

The next morning, I put on the shirt, excited to wear it to school, although I was certain no one else would understand or even care. My peers were too busy listening to a bunch of rap artists I'd never heard of, and folk music was not exactly on their radar. This didn't concern me, though. That morning, I was still on cloud nine from the night before, remembering the songs she'd played on her ever-present blue-black Taylor guitar. I drifted through my first three classes, reliving every moment of the best concert I'd ever been to.

After French class, I came down the stairs to find the usually bustling cafeteria dead silent. All the TVs around the room were turned to the news, where the Twin Towers were collapsing on repeat. My dreamlike daze flatlined, replaced by mind-numbing fear and unanswerable questions. How could something so horrible happen after everything had been so magnificent?

It was the beginning of an awful year. I was already struggling with depression, and the terrifying aftermath of the national tragedy only accelerated its progression. Not long after this, I became the target of emotional abuse and isolation from classmates, which thrust me into loneliness and exacerbated my poor mental health. Fearful of rejection, I tightened into myself even more, curling like a potato bug in the sunlight. It reached a point where I seemed to be detached from everything going on around me and was merely existing, each day an exhausting struggle to get through. The world was a place of darkness and evil, and it had forgotten me.

The only thing that consistently brought me comfort was Nanci Griffith.

One of my favorite songs on *Clock Without Hands* was "Midnight in Missoula." In it, the speaker recalls a faraway loved one, imagining the person's life and what she might be doing at that moment. The song's wistful blend of guitar and piano brought me such warmth and comfort that I'd often lie in bed with my CD Walkman next to my pillow, the song programmed to play on repeat. I imagined Nanci singing to me, the music wrapping around me like a cocoon. The song was a gift, a lullaby for a scared sixteen-year-old who felt alone and forsaken. Nanci stepped into every empty place in my life, filling every void with a balm for the hollowness.

After Nanci passed away in 2021, I learned that she wrote "Midnight in Missoula" for her goddaughter, Julia. Nanci once stayed with Julia's family for Christmas, and it was that trip that inspired her to write the song. The lyrics suggest that it was a special, intimate time—there are references to climbing a hill and surveying the lights of the city, of hearing the speaker's loved one, perhaps Julia herself, play the viola. But eventually, that holiday season ended, Nanci departed for her extensive travels as a musician, and it is evident from the song that she missed Julia desperately. After Nanci's passing, Julia posted a picture online of the two of them standing on her family's front porch, with the doorway framed by Christmas lights and the falling snow sparkling in the camera lens, just as the song describes. Nanci and Julia, clad in winter coats, stand together, arms around each other, smiling.

During that year when the security of my life and the world around me caved in from all directions, I often felt like I belonged to no one, as if I were drifting like snow, only to settle, unnoticed, in someplace colder than I'd left. Few things could restore my sense of belonging. But Nanci Griffith, whom I would only ever know through her music, entered my life at times when things felt darkest and most desolate. Like Julia, I felt her cling to me as that song's pensive melody wrapped itself around my shoulders like a thick blanket, reminding me that I was safe and that there were still good and beautiful things in the world.

In these days of fear and division, of wars and rumors of wars, her music *still* does.

WHY THE SHAWSHANK REDEMPTION IS MY FAVORITE MOVIE

The letter-writing campaign finally paid off. Andy Dufresne got the money from the State Department of Finance to fund the expansion of the Shawshank Prison library, plus boxes and boxes of books and records donated from local book clubs. These are now piled up in the main office, and he's been tasked with clearing them out before the warden returns.

Andy is flipping through the albums when he comes across a recording of Mozart's *Le Nozze di Figaro*. A thin smile spreads across his face. You can tell it's his favorite, and since he's been in prison for ten years, it's been a while since he's heard it.

The office has a record player, and his supervising guard is reading a *Jughead* comic book on the toilet, so Andy puts the album on. The orchestral opening wafts from the speakers and a woman begins to sing in Italian. A wistful expression crosses his face—*a memory?*—and he stands there, frozen, listening to the notes well up like tears.

Startled, the guard calls out to Andy from the bathroom. It's then that Andy's idea takes shape. You can see it in his eyes. He locks both the bathroom and office doors, then turns on the intercom and positions the microphone in front of the record player's speaker.

There's a startling squeal of feedback, and then the music comes through clearly as a second woman's voice joins in. All over the prison grounds, people hear them—orderlies in the infirmary, prisoners laboring in the woodshop, groups of men smoking contraband cigarettes in the exercise yard. Everything stops. There is nothing, no inch of Shawshank State Prison, that their voices do not cover.

Meanwhile, Andy props up his feet and leans back into the office's desk chair as if listening to the opera on the hi-fi in his living room. By this point, the warden is out in the hall, beating on the glassed-in door and threatening to smash it open. Andy ignores him. His pugnacious face contorted in anger, the warden warns Andy repeatedly to turn the music off and open the door. Andy pauses and reaches for the tonearm. For a moment, it seems like he might listen, but then, his hand moves to the volume knob instead. He gets a week in solitary confinement—what the inmates call "the hole"—but you can tell he considers it a worthy sacrifice.

When Andy emerges, he tells his friends that the music was there with him as he sat alone in the dank, pitch-dark cell. One convict asks if he'd found such favor with the guards that they let him lug the record player down there. Andy shakes his head and grins. The music was inside him, he says, the hope they couldn't take away.

There is defiance in the love of beauty, in sharing it despite the bleakness of the world and despite the risks, because in the end, those things don't matter and are passing away. In the face of such splendor, darkness has no choice but to flee.

THIS IS MY BODY

1

I was visiting my grandmother's church the first time I heard the word *communion*. I was seven, and my only association with a plate of crackers and juice being passed around was snack time at school. I eagerly reached for the tray as it came to our pew.

My grandmother smacked my wrist. It was more shocking than painful. *That's not for you*, she whispered through clenched teeth.

Perhaps that moment shaped how I first saw Christ—unapproachable, distant, something I could not touch.

2

During grad school, I was scared to go to church. I had been saved two years before, and I still couldn't believe that after a lifetime of staunch atheism and outright mocking of Christians, I had now become one. The idea of being forgiven of my sins purely by God's grace, not anything I'd done to make myself acceptable to him, was still too surreal to grasp. My salvation was like a small glass bird, and I feared that if I let too many people into my conversion, they would play rough with it and break it.

So, a friend and I did communion over the phone. I used club crackers and real wine in a shot glass with my university's logo on it. He read the traditional texts from 1 Corinthians and Matthew. My mind always got snagged on the last verse: *I will not drink henceforth of this fruit of the vine, until that day when I drink it new with you in my Father's kingdom.*[1] Though I was young in my faith and did not yet understand what Jesus meant by the Kingdom, I knew that the cup I drank was a foretaste of something greater. I would someday stand in his presence, face to face, and together we would partake of new wine.

The words of scripture came from a thousand miles away but strengthened my newfound belief, this mystery that was still taking root.

3

When I finally joined a church a year later, we held communion at tables around the elementary school gym where we gathered for services. Each was covered in a white tablecloth with the bread (pasty wafers) and the wine (Welch's grape juice) on a gold plate in the center. We gathered around the table, like the disciples had, with the church elders administering the elements.

I stood at the table, the man I would someday marry on one side and the pastor who would officiate at our wedding on the other. I listened to him recite the words of scripture—*the Lord Jesus on the night when he was betrayed took bread . . .*[2]

In that moment, we were united. We were of one mind. But someday, another congregation would rend love into scraps of judgment and shame, making Christ as distant to me as before I knew Him.

---

1 Matt. 26:29 KJV
2 1 Cor. 11:23 ESV

4

We stepped in tentatively. Church, by nature, is communal. How do we *not forsake the assembling of yourselves together*[3] three months into a pandemic?

We had a parking lot service. The praise team and the pastor of the church we now belonged to were set up on a makeshift stage outside. The parking lot itself was packed, the cars all lined up with their windows down as if we were at a drive-in movie. We were so thrilled to be together after so many weeks of quarantine and Facebook Live services that it never struck us how unnatural this was.

During the service, one of the deaconesses went from car to car, passing out prepackaged communion cups—peel back the top, and there's a wafer; peel back the next layer, and there's juice. We listened to the pastor recite the passage through our car radios via a short-range transmitter—*This is my body, given for you.*[4] We broke the spongy wafers in two and drank the juice, which tasted like watery Jell-O.

Perhaps it was appropriate—a way to engage, partake, and draw close, although we could not touch.

---

3   Heb. 10:25 KJV
4   Luke 22:19 NIV

CLOSER TO FINE

I was hanging out with a friend in the apartment I rented during my last year of college when he told me I could be a Christian and still like the Indigo Girls. It was one of many conversations we'd had over the last year about the nature of suffering, creation, redemption, and God. I was a longtime atheist, but something was changing. Whenever people spoke about Jesus, my brain felt like it was cracking like concrete uprooted by the growth of trees.

"I'm ambivalent," I said. "Sometimes I think I really could become a Christian. But I just don't think it's possible."

"Why not?" He leaned forward and looked at me, concerned, like he was expecting me to confess a secret sin, something too awful or humiliating for God to ever accept.

I took a deep breath. "It's because of my music. If I became a Christian, I'd have to stop listening to my angry girl folk music."

His face scrunched up in confusion. "Angry girl . . . folk music?"

"Yeah, you know. Liz Phair, the Blake Babies, the Indigo Girls—God would never approve of any of that."

It seems laughable, but to me, this was a big deal. During my junior year of high school, a friend gave me a copy of the Indigo Girls' debut album. I put it in the three-disc CD changer in my room, then sat on the bed and listened as the opening chords of "Closer to Fine" leaped out of the speakers and wrapped me in a fierce hug. In the first few lines, Emily Saliers sang about trying to tell people about her life, and the words pierced me. It seemed like all I ever did was try to tell people about my life—the anger and sadness I couldn't shake, the loneliness and isolation I felt at school, the dark, hopeless life I seemed trapped in while everyone else seemed totally fine. Nobody would listen. Nobody seemed to care.

But the Indigo Girls did. The more I delved into their catalog, the more I felt this kinship. Their songs ranged from guitar-driven expulsions of anger to quiet reflections of angst and sadness. They wrote songs about rejection and spiritual confusion and betrayal. In every manifestation of their music, they seemed to understand me when so few people even tried to.

Whenever music speaks to me, it becomes a part of me. Like antibodies, it rushes toward the sick and broken places and surrounds them, reclaiming them for itself. But my love for the Indigo Girls' music was so tied to my intense feelings of frustration and unbelonging that I wondered how there could be a place for it in my life if I were a Christian. Surely, it was a part of me that God could never accept. After all, isn't everything that isn't righteous supposed to just vanish after you believe?

My friend was quiet. He ran the toe of his sneaker along my blue and yellow shag carpet, seeming baffled about how to respond. Then he glanced up at me, a saddened look in his eyes. "Is that really what you think?" he said.

"I mean, yeah. If I became a Christian, that would be the end. All my Indigo Girls CDs. In a bonfire."

"Wait a minute." He seemed indignant but also looked like he was trying not to laugh. "You think Jesus is going to reject you because of a band you like? C'mon. That's not how salvation works."

He explained again the facts he'd spoken to me over and over about sin separating me from a holy God and Jesus's death on the cross being my payment and being saved by grace through faith. I still didn't get it. But now, one fact was blatantly apparent.

"So, I could be a Christian *and* like the Indigo Girls?" I felt my mouth hanging slightly open. This was revelatory.

My friend laughed at my enthusiasm. Salvation, he explained, is a free gift that only requires faith. Add any other requirement—even something as small as having to burn your Indigo Girls CDs—and it goes from being a gift to something you have to earn. Given the tremendous sacrifice that Jesus made, it would be the same as saying that his death on the cross, which paid the penalty for our sins in total, was for nothing.[1]

That wasn't to say, he added, that my tastes in music wouldn't change as I grew in my faith. Becoming more like Christ doesn't happen in an instant—it's a process, one that lasts your whole life. Like a sculptor unveiling the image hidden in a block of stone, God is constantly working to chisel away pieces that no longer serve a purpose so his image can be more clearly seen. It might become apparent to me as I matured spiritually that a story or song that I used to love would no longer mean as much as it once did.

But God is patient. It happens in his time, not ours. And when he ordains change in our lives, it is always for the purpose of making us more like Jesus.

I could feel myself smiling, and he chuckled slightly at my enthusiasm. "So yeah. You can still like your angry girl folk music." He grinned. "You know you can receive Christ right now. If you want, I mean. No pressure. Or we can just go get pizza. It's up to you."

I chose the pizza. I was curious, but I wasn't ready and wouldn't be for some time. Still, I don't think he realized what he'd just done. He'd removed a huge obstacle that I didn't even know had stood in my way.

It wasn't just knowing I could still like the Indigo Girls, although that was a big part of it. More importantly, it was the first time someone had told me that being a Christian didn't mean losing myself. God wants every part of us, not just the attributes of ourselves that we think are acceptable to him. What is even better is that the transformation that comes with believing in Christ is

---

1   "I do not nullify the grace of God, for if righteousness were through the law, then Christ died for no purpose." (Gal. 2:21 ESV)

his doing: "*And we all, with unveiled face, beholding the glory of the Lord, are being transformed into the same image from one degree of glory to another.*"[2]

The change he brings about can only come from beholding him.

I now know that these blessings are far greater than music, and that the new identity we receive at the moment of salvation transcends any concerns about what artists are acceptable to listen to. My friend was also right—almost twenty years later, although I still like my angry girl folk music, there are other artists and types of music that I prefer. Spiritual maturity simply means that the more years you spend upon Christ, the less the things of the world that you cling to will matter.

But in that moment, I knew that if I ever became a Christian, I would do so with my Indigo Girls CDs intact. It would be a long time before God gave me the desire to turn to him. Until then, I was comforted by knowing that stepping toward him did not mean stepping away from the music that held meaning for me in the broken spaces where I'd lived.

---

2   2 Cor. 3:18 ESV

VERILY, VERILY, I SAY UNTO THEE

A friend I hadn't seen in some time was passing through and asked if he could make a detour to the small college I attended. He wanted to take me out to dinner at Texas Roadhouse. The food at my school cafeteria was not good, so I of course wanted to exchange manufactured steak or a night out at Taco Bell for a genuine ribeye and rolls with honey butter.

At the restaurant, I got a Coke, and he ordered a Dos Equis. Cracking open the shells of peanuts from a metal bucket on the table, we chit chatted about my literary criticism and American lit classes and books I was reading. Most notably, we discussed my latest draft of the novel I was writing for my senior thesis. It was about the Carter Family's 1927 recording sessions with Victor Records in Bristol, Virginia, where they contributed to what music historians call "The Big Bang of Country Music."

As a long-time country music fan, my friend was enthusiastic about the project and wanted to help me get the details right. He told me the amount of research I'd done for the book and my commitment to authenticity were impressive, but we had a problem. A major one. The main characters were Christians, and all of my theology was wrong. If I wanted to portray these people's lives authentically, I needed to flesh out the characters' beliefs more and make them a bigger part of the story.

I balked at this. I had no desire to write about Christian characters, but my fascination with the Carter Family made it a worthy trade-off. And he wasn't wrong—Christianity had played a role in every aspect of their lives, especially their music. Most of the songs they recorded were either hymns or inspired by scripture, and writing about their faith was unavoidable. My friend reassured me that he was just trying to make the book more realistic. It was not an attempt to convert me.

Better not be, I thought. I ripped the shell off another peanut and threw it on the ground.

My friend took a napkin from the dispenser on the table and pulled a Pilot pen out of his pocket. He drew a cross with a squiggly line weaved through it. There was a story that went with the image, he said. The people of Israel were dying from a plague of vicious snakes as a result of their ungratefulness for God's provision. God declared that the only way for them to be saved from the plague was for Moses to craft a bronze serpent and lift it up on a pole. Anyone who looked upon the serpent would be healed and protected.

Nice story, I said, but I didn't understand what it had to do with my book or what my characters would have believed.

He took a drink before opening a pocket New Testament. He started to read to me from John 3, but I objected. I already knew the John 3 stuff—"for God so loved the world" and whatnot, which still made no sense to me because all God seemed to do was hate the world, allowing death, mental illness, terrorist attacks, and school shootings, all of which he theoretically had the power to stop, which was why I couldn't believe in him and why I wished my friend would please, please, *please* stop trying.

He acknowledged my objections but told me to please just pipe down for a minute and listen. Then, he told me about the Jewish ruler named Nicodemus, who was so curious to speak with Jesus that he met with him in secret under the cover of night. The rest of the Jewish leaders saw Jesus as a threat to their power, so no one could know that Nicodemus had gone to see him.

I don't know what Nicodemus expected to hear when he said he knew Jesus was a teacher sent by God, but surely, he didn't anticipate what happened next. Jesus told his people's story back to him, a picture of the Messiah's coming death on the cross: *And as Moses lifted up the serpent in the wilderness, even so must the Son of man be lifted up.*[1]

Then, at our table in the restaurant, with Tim McGraw playing in the background and the sound of chatter from people drinking at the bar, something clicked in my head. The metaphor. The same image from Exodus, given new meaning in the life of Christ: the God-Man lifted up to bring rescue and protection from death for all who would look upon him.

This new detail captured my attention in a way that the John 3:16 message hadn't before. I knew my friend had done this on purpose. He picked that passage because I was an English major and, therefore, a sucker for figurative language.

Part of me was irritated by this. The rest was too spellbound to care. I'd never really read the Bible before. I didn't know it told stories. I thought all it did was yell at you and tell you how much you'd messed up your life.

I asked to see the pocket New Testament. I read the words for myself, set in red against the thin, cream-colored paper. *Verily, verily, I say unto thee, Except a man be born again, he cannot see the Kingdom of God.*[2]

As we ate dinner, my friend told me that if I wanted to, I could leave the Texas Roadhouse and our beer-stained, peanut-shell-dusted table having received Jesus as my Savior. Thinking back, I find this humorous, even absurd by some evangelical standards. Conversion moments aren't supposed to happen at Texas Roadhouse. It's supposed to be like a scene from one of those faith-based movies: in a garden with an arched, white trellis and perfectly arranged flowers. Violin-swelled background music plays as a mediocre actor

---

1 John 3:14 KJV
2 John 3:3 KJV

shares the gospel with me, reaching its crescendo as we tearfully embrace, and I ask Jesus to come into my heart.

But that isn't real life.

Real life is cracked peanut shells and country music playing over the speakers at the Texas Roadhouse.

Real life is the bronze serpent drawn on a Coors napkin.

Real life is that the heart is deceitful above all things and desperately wicked.[3]

And in that moment of real life, I said no because, like Nicodemus, I was too afraid to come into the light.

But back in my dorm room that night, I stared at the ceiling, thinking of the bronze serpent on the pole and the healing of the Israelites, the lilting words of John 3 running through my brain: *verily, verily, I say unto thee.*

And for the first time, I wondered if it all was true.

---

3   Jer. 17:9 KJV

GOD'S GONNA CUT YOU DOWN

The first thing I did when I moved into my first apartment in college was hang up an enormous poster of Johnny Cash's famous photo from his concert at San Quentin—the one where he's making a lewd gesture at the photographer, sneering defiantly. It took up most of the main wall in the living room. As my dad helped me move in, he eyed it with disgust. He asked if I wanted *that* to be the first thing people saw when they came into my apartment and if I'd considered what they would think about me.

I told him they would think I liked Johnny Cash.

About an hour later, one of my neighbors in the house stopped by to welcome me. His name was Jon, and he and his roommate, Mark, lived in the attic apartment. We made small talk, gradually moving from the narrow hallway into my living room.

When he saw the poster, Jon's jaw dropped. "Hey, man!" he exclaimed. "Johnny Cash! All right!"

I shot my dad a look. He grunted and kept hooking up my TV.

I've been a Johnny Cash fan since I first heard the album *At Folsom Prison* in high school. His iconic, forceful baritone immediately grabbed my attention, and I loved the way his songs show the best and worst of humanity with brutal honesty and grit. But no Cash music has meant more to me than the American Recordings albums produced by the legendary Rick Rubin. The humility of Cash's ragged, aging voice as he covers U2, Gordon Lightfoot, Simon and Garfunkel, Soundgarden, and dozens of hymns reveals the core of who he was as an artist and his ability to make any song his own. He didn't just become a part of the history of the piece. He sang it with such stark authenticity that you can tell the song itself became a part of him.

American IV: The Man Comes Around, which features his searing cover of Trent Reznor's "Hurt," should have been his final album, as he passed away several months after its release in 2003. But shortly after I moved into the apartment and the school year began, Rubin announced that Cash had completed one last record before his death. Music was the only way he knew to cope with the loss of his wife, June Carter Cash, and overwhelmed by grief, he went back into the studio for the last months of his life. These new songs were the product of those sessions. *American V: A Hundred Highways* was coming out that fall.

I bought the album on release day, then sat back in my blue bean bag chair in the living room to enjoy Cash's final offering. The cover featured a blurred, black-and-white image of his frail face as he solemnly leaned into a microphone. I listened to the whole record four or five times, transfixed by his haunting voice, obviously weathered by grief and age.

At some point, Jon came and knocked on my door. Strains of the album drifted into the hallway, and he grinned in recognition. He told me he and Mark had been playing it all day too. In fact, that's why he'd stopped by. They had a Bible study in their attic every Tuesday night and wanted to know if I'd like to come.

I told him I didn't really "do" Bible studies. My feelings about God had become complicated over the last year, and I didn't want to spoil the mood. But Jon told me that the focus of the study that night was going to be *American V*. The group would listen to the album and talk about whatever biblical topics arose from the experience. I might not be a Christian, he said, but I was a huge Johnny Cash fan, and therefore, my perspective would be valuable.

I could get into that.

That night, I climbed the narrow staircase to Jon and Mark's apartment. The attic was packed with guys from the Christian fraternity, most of whom I already knew. I went to their parties because they were the only dry frat on campus, and I felt safe there. Moreover, most of them were English majors, and we had a shared love of books, stories, and even movies. They knew I didn't believe in God, but they never condemned me and never asked me to justify myself. They said they understood.

I'd never had people who said they were Christians try to understand me before.

We hunkered down in the small living room and listened to the whole album, Cash's deep voice reverberating through the attic's thin walls. Listening to it with other people was different, almost as if I were hearing it for the first time. The heavy drum beat on "God's Gonna Cut You Down," like footsteps echoing down the hall of a prison cell block, resonated through the room as he sang about the perils of running from Jesus, that no matter how hard you try to get away, we all must someday give an account to him. We all have sinned, and sin demands punishment. There are no exceptions.

I understood none of this at the time, though I knew it was related to the righteous judgment of the God I did not believe in, yet was struggling to understand. But even though I'd listened to the song several times already, hearing the lyrics at that moment gave me an eerie sense of discomfort. I tried to tell myself it was just religion, the kind of thing I didn't believe in, a bunch of myths my friends had bought into that I was too smart to accept.

Still, being in that room, with its low ceiling and slanted shadows of lamplight, made the message more potent. It was like hearing a ghost story about a haunted house I'd just moved into. And because Johnny Cash was singing the song, it carried more weight—a sense of authority that made those myths seem nearer to reality.

When the album was over, the group talked about the songs, liner notes and Bibles open next to each other. I don't recall the specifics of what anyone said. I just sat there and listened as they made connections that I couldn't understand at the time. I just let them in, like watching a foreign film without subtitles, absorbing as much of the meaning as I could.

A couple of months later, it would all make sense. God would catch up to me. The words Cash sang would become real. I would understand the truth wrapped inside the voice and songs I admired, and their meaning would multiply into something transformative.

But that time had not yet come.

When the study was over, I thanked Jon and Mark for inviting me and returned to my apartment, to the watchful, sneering eyes of Johnny Cash on my wall.

OWL WALK

We crept into the woods at night, the lights of the nature preserve dormitory fading to pinpricks the deeper we ventured in. We were hunting for owls. It was a weekend-long expedition for our geology class, and our professor said the preserve grounds were replete with owls in mid-October. So, we tightened our jackets around us in the night chill, flashlights in hand, and followed him up the wooded trail, our beams of light darting in the dark.

The professor held aloft an iPod with a small speaker stuck in the headphone jack, which emitted the sounds of the Eastern screech and barn owls. The volume was cranked all the way up, but we could barely hear the synthetic hoots and swooshes. Neither, we imagined, could the owls. We stood shoulder to shoulder in a pack while the muted cries drifted into the dark, our flashlights pointed to the ground.

There was not much to think about while waiting for the appearance of one of the fabled owls. Instead of merely staring at the withered bush next to me on the path, I thought of the God I did not believe in. The geology course had made me wonder about creation, made it more real to me. I saw the intricacies of the bands of fossils, the incredible force that different minerals exuded against each other, and wondered whether glaciers and canyons and end moraines and waterfalls were not formed by accident as I'd always believed, but had been designed through careful artistry, using water and pressure and time as tools the way a master sculptor uses chisels and hammers.

I saw the night around us as a shadow of the time when *the earth was without form, and void,*[1] the cold and the damp transporting me to when there was nothing but God, who was preparing to blast the darkness apart with his command for light, for the moment when the emptiness would shatter, and all that he'd imagined would burst into being.

---

1   Gen. 1:2 KJV

WISE BLOOD

During my first meeting with my academic advisor at the start of my senior year of college, he threw a copy of *The Complete Stories of Flannery O'Connor* across his desk at me. I was a creative writing major but had only read two of her stories, and he was horrified. It was bad enough that I was unfamiliar with her larger body of work, but I was also applying for Master of Fine Arts programs in creative writing, and in his eyes, a lack of basic O'Connor knowledge made me woefully unprepared.

He ordered me to take the book home and said he didn't want to see my face in his office again until I'd finished reading it. Besides, he added, he knew it was going to open up a whole new way of looking at my craft. He grinned at me as I walked out the door.

I was only a few pages into the book when I learned something about Flannery O'Connor that astounded me. Ever since I'd read "A Good Man is Hard to Find," one of her most anthologized stories, back in high school, I'd labored under the notion that she was not only an atheist but also an embittered, crotchety old Irishman. After all, the author seemed intent on calling out the main character, an elderly, self-centered woman, as a religious hypocrite, and the brutal ending, which involves a serial killer murdering a family on the side of a road, struck me as a cynical depiction of life's futility.

Conversely, the introduction, penned by her editor Robert Giroux, described Flannery as a young, devoutly Catholic woman with a sharp wit and a wry sense of humor who died at age thirty-nine after a long battle with lupus.

This new knowledge was shocking. The way I saw it back then, no one who believed in God could write stories so harsh and abrasive, and for that matter, no woman could either. But as I read through the book, Flannery enlarged my perspective. I had always thought that Christian authors only wrote syrupy, overly emotional tales that ended with people falling to their knees and proclaiming that Jesus is Lord. I was already angry with God, and the self-serving piety of faith-based fiction and movies only made it worse.

Yet, in spite of its obvious religious themes of sin and grace, I was delighted to find that her fiction was gloriously dark. The stories were populated with murderers, false prophets, and self-righteous religious women who frequently have to reckon with their double-mindedness, often in intensely emotional and even deadly ways. They are gored by bulls, get physically attacked, and have dramatic visions that reveal the consequences of thinking too highly of one's self. I wasn't a believer, but something about these characters felt like a more sincere portrayal of Christianity than the sickeningly sweet stories I was accustomed to.

When I saw my advisor again the next week, he was pleased that I liked Flannery's work as much as he'd predicted. He told me my next step was to read her first novel, *Wise Blood*. The copy I purchased from Amazon was an out-of-print edition with a blue and red cover depicting a human heart wrapped in barbed wire. I read voraciously for two days, consumed by the story of Hazel Motes, a young man who has returned from war to the emptiness and loneliness of his past and haunting memories of his abusive, fanatically religious grandfather. Surveying the detritus of his life, Hazel concludes that Jesus isn't real. If he were, Hazel concludes, God would intervene in his circumstances and his life would look very different.

In view of this conclusion, Hazel creates his own religion, the Church Without Christ, whose central truth is that Jesus never lived, died, or rose from the dead because there is no such thing as sin. The hope of the human race is that there is no hope, this life is all there is, and we have the freedom to enjoy what time we have without fear of judgment. To enlist new converts, Hazel buys a broken-down car and drives around town proclaiming his new non-faith by preaching from the car's roof, dressed in a blue suit and a black hat.

As I read *Wise Blood*, I identified with Hazel in a way that was more potent than how I connected with Flannery's other characters. I did not believe in Jesus for all the same reasons as Hazel. I looked at the horror of the world and saw no evidence of a compassionate creator. I'd also been hurt by a hypocritical, religious grandparent who spent my childhood humiliating me and degrading my family for not being good Christians like her. Moreover, I had always struggled with depression, spiritual angst, and a pervasive feeling that there was nowhere that I belonged.

Therefore, as bizarre as it seems, Hazel's beliefs gave me a perverse sense of comfort. *Wise Blood* gave me hope that I was okay after all, and that perhaps Flannery even understood, despite her Christianity, that the idea of a loving, all-present God had limitations for some people.

But, of course, that's not what the book is about.

As the story goes on, Hazel's efforts become more hysterical and desperate. A rival preacher co-opts the Church Without Christ, encroaches on Hazel's territory in his own dilapidated car, accompanied by a man dressed in Hazel's signature hat and suit, whom he refers to as a prophet. Hazel responds to this threat by forcing the prophet to take off his clothes and running him over with his car. While attempting to skip town after the murder, Hazel's slowly disintegrating car gives up the ghost, and as a dramatic underscore of his situation, a police officer who finds him stranded on the side of the road pushes it down a hill, where it crashes at the bottom.

Hazel is left with nothing except the realization that the Jesus he's tried so desperately to run from has finally caught up to him.

Sin is real—without the trappings of his false religion, he can see the full extent of his ugliness. But his pride still is too great for him to fall at the feet of Christ. Instead, he blinds himself and wraps his body in barbed wire, trying to take upon himself the penalty that only Christ is able to pay. His blindness leaves him unable to care for himself, yet he spurns his landlady's offer to marry him and give him a comfortable home, instead choosing to be homeless. Unwilling to accept either the grace of Christ or the grace of this woman, he dies from exposure.

When I finished the novel, I sat on the edge of my bed, staring at the cover's stark image of the barbed-wire heart. It was not the book I thought it was.

Flannery O'Connor was not an atheist. Hazel Motes was a false prophet. And I, too, was haunted by Jesus, whom I was increasingly beginning to believe was real. I couldn't outrun him. It was only a matter of time before he caught up to me and forced me to look at my own deformed, wire-wrapped, horribly defective heart.

The contrast between Hazel and me, of course, is that we made different choices. Hazel chose to atone for his own sins, and in doing so, he chose spiritual death. I chose to stop running and surrender to Christ, who paid my debt for me.

Fiction, of course, does not replace God's holy and inspired Word. Reading the scriptures was what ultimately confirmed my sinful state before God and my need to be saved. But without *Wise Blood*, I wouldn't have been prepared to open the Bible for the purpose of investigating the state of my own soul. Although manmade stories have limitations, they are often the crucial domino that needs to be poked in order for our false conceptions of truth to collapse one by one.

Several years after I was born again, I read the prayer journal Flannery kept while pursuing her Master of Fine Arts in creative writing. In one entry, she desperately pleads for God to make her a good writer and to help her glorify him by writing a truly excellent novel—the book that would become *Wise Blood*.

I imagine her sitting at a scuffed-up desk in the graduate dormitory at the University of Iowa, still adjusting to the cold temperatures after a lifetime spent in Georgia, furiously scribbling in a composition notebook as she pours out her creative frustrations to God, praying for the novel that he would someday use to humble me.

I Didn't Become a Christian Because of My Near-Death Experience

This had already happened once before. The tightening in my throat, like swallowing a pill that's too big; the puffiness in my face; the tender swelling of my lips, which are fat like cocktail sausages. For over a month, I've been fighting *dermatographia*, an auto-immune disease that attacks the skin, making me allergic to the world, embossing its patterns on my body in blood-red hives.

But now, for reasons my multitude of doctors can't explain, it's affecting my internal tissues. It's become life-threatening.

Last time, the symptoms evolved slowly. Providentially, I was on the phone with a friend who was a doctor when it happened. He asked how I was holding up, and I told him I felt okay, except that my throat wouldn't stop itching. He cut off the conversation and ordered me to go to the ER. If we hadn't been on that call, I might have never known anything was wrong and just suffocated in my apartment.

But this time, I know better. This time, it's worse. The flare-up is progressing more quickly; the tickling sensation in my throat and lips is rapidly giving way to something more treacherous.

I call my friend Mike. I need to go to the hospital. Now.

Our college is in the middle of a cornfield, and the hospital is a half hour away. Mike guns it down the long, lightless country road until we reach the nearest town, then swerves up to the ER entrance, hits the brakes with a screech, and drops me off. The attending nurse takes one look at my exploding face and ushers me down the hall to a curtained-off bed.

I can barely talk. By this time, Mike is with me and can explain to her what's going on. She prepares some plastic tubes and needles. My chest tightens. I've never had an IV before, and I squirm and squeal as she disinfects my arm. I'm terrified that the needle will come dislodged and blood will shoot all over the room. Mike holds my hand and mutters that I need to stay with him, to breathe, that it's all going to be fine.

The IV contains steroids to reduce the swelling, as well as Benadryl and Ativan. I've been on Ativan before for anxiety, and I know it won't be long before it alone puts me in a stupor. Mike asks me if I'm okay. Referencing George Costanza after his botched visit to the new age healer on *Seinfeld*, I tell him I'm an eggplant. Then I conk out.

I stay in a twilight sleep for several hours. I hallucinate that my nurse is the girl who lives downstairs from me, with whom I'd been studying for a geology exam earlier that day. I carry on an incoherent conversation with her about dinosaurs. I can still feel the tightness in my throat, but the daze from the Ativan and Benadryl has made it not matter as much.

In one strange moment of lucidity, I realize I might be dying. I think of my friends who have told me I need to repent and believe in Jesus Christ, the peculiar push and pull I've felt when I've thought about grace and forgiveness.

If I were going to become a Christian, now would be the time. But I can't bring myself to do it. It wouldn't be honest. God would know I was lying, that I was just mouthing the words out of fear. I'd rather go to hell than lie to him.

Years later, I realized this was the moment I first believed that God was real.

Around six in the morning, the doctor on duty says the swelling has subsided, and I'm free to go. My throat has loosened up, and I can talk again. The swelling in my face is gone. I'm not an eggplant. I'm not going to die—not today, anyway.

When I tell people this story, they always assume it's why I became a Christian. I know sometimes it's like that for people, being confronted with the inevitability of death. But that didn't happen to me. If anything did happen that night, it's that I afforded God the dignity and glory he deserves by giving him honesty instead of a lie.

THE WOMAN WITH THE ISSUE
OF BLOOD

Aside from Jesus Christ, I think about her more than anyone else in scripture. Of course, I have the obvious questions: Who was she? What was her name? How old was she, or, given the nature of her infirmity, how young?

These are things the Scriptures do not tell us. We know she suffered from this affliction for twelve years and that she was destitute from spending money on doctors who did not help her but instead made her symptoms worse.

But there is one more pressing question that comes to my mind: What did it *feel* like?

I remember the worst period I ever had. I was on vacation with my mom, lying in the hotel room with a warm compress she borrowed from the woman at the front desk. The sharp pain stabbed at my abdomen, bringing with it waves of nausea as blood and flesh tugged downward. When I think of the unnamed woman with the issue of blood, I multiply my afternoon of relative discomfort into days, weeks, months, and years of agonizing pain with no heating pads or Midol. I imagine relentless body aches and endless fatigue from iron deficiency.

And then there's the mess. I try to imagine not owning a single piece of clothing that isn't covered in the decay of dried, brown stains while living with primitive and ill-equipped bathing facilities. No sanitary products. Being constantly followed by the salty, earthy scent of fresh blood, leaving a trail of it in my wake.

All of this would be bad enough. But it isn't even the worst part.

This woman would have lived a life of complete isolation. She would have been declared unclean by the Jewish priests and forbidden to make sacrifices at the Temple or to worship God there. She would have been treated as a leper, watching people avert their eyes in disgust whenever she passed by.

We know the next part best: in desperation, she went to see Jesus as he passed through her village. There was a thick, pressing crowd. People would have been shoving her away, calling her names. The bloody stench would have been magnified by the heat of the day and the volume of people clamoring for his attention. Resolved, she made her way through the crowd, and when Jesus passed by, she reached out and touched the hem of his garment, believing that if she could simply do that, she would be healed. And she was, instantly.

This is the part that is hardest to imagine: what it would have been like to suffer so long, to endure so much judgment and seclusion, only to have it all suddenly and miraculously ended by a man who looks into your eyes and says, "Daughter, your faith has made you well; go in peace."[1]

In the fall of my senior year of college, I went on a weekend trip with my geology class. We gathered around a fire pit one night in the bowl of a deep valley, wrapped against the autumn chill.

---

1   Luke 8:48 ESV

Sitting on a wet log, pulling away the crisp shell of a marshmallow with my teeth, I felt the back of my thighs begin to tingle, then itch, then burn. Later, I discovered that the burning skin was covered with scarlet, amoeba-shaped hives. I rubbed the affected area with hydrocortisone cream and hoped it would go away.

It didn't.

In the weeks that followed, I woke up every morning covered in thick, raised welts. I felt them as soon as I became conscious— uncomfortable tickles, like leeches clinging to my skin. Over the next three months, I saw at least six doctors, who ran tests for lupus, rheumatoid arthritis, cancer, and other terrifying outcomes, but all the results were negative. The best diagnosis they could come up with was *dermatographia*. Latin for "skin writing."

Dermatographia is an autoimmune disease that makes your body paranoid. It mistakes everything in your environment for a threat, firing off squads of neurotic antibodies at the brush of your own clothing, the accidental shove of a stranger in public, the scratch of your fingers to relieve your skin's never-ending itching. It pens the narrative of your world on your body in hives, and the moment they fade, new ones appear as you come into contact with the next perceived enemy.

Often, those who suffer from this condition never find out the cause. Technically, I am among them, although I'm certain that my case was the result of mold in the walls of the slum house where I rented an apartment that year. The kitchen periodically smelled sulfuric and rotten, and one night during a power outage, I discovered six inches of standing water in the basement while looking for the fuse box. Several years after I moved out, the house was demolished due to significant structural damage.

Regardless, I spent the next two months in ongoing discomfort. Along with the hives, my joints ached, and I had to ration my energy to complete my assignments and graduate school applications due to constant fatigue. My body's internal temperature was confused; I either had hot flashes or deep, penetrating chills. Twice, I went to the hospital for anaphylaxis in my throat. The only treatment these doctors could prescribe was two courses of steroids, which only compounded the symptoms, worsening the swelling in my body. I once went to a doctor's appointment in bedroom slippers, unable to wear shoes with my swollen feet. Finally, I began to wonder if I was going to die, if the applications and graduation requirements I worked so hard on would ever see fruit.

Eventually, my ongoing questions about Christianity and my hopelessness regarding my illness drove me to read the Bible. My friends at the Christian frat and other people who had been sharing the Gospel with me told me it had all the answers. Despite my remaining skepticism, I was at the end of my rope, so I began to read through the Gospels, searching for some explanation about why this might be happening to me.

Then, one night, stricken with chills, the hives crawling up my legs and encircling my body, I met the woman with the issue of blood.

The story leaped off the pages of Luke, bombarding me with empathy. I was stymied by the striking similarities between our situations: the loneliness, the desperation, and the healing that came from her act of courage.

But there was more to the passage than just these parallels. According to Jesus, the reality of my physical sickness was bad enough, but the prognosis of my spiritual condition was worse than I could have imagined. I was terminally ill with sin, and it made me dirty, messy, and weak in all respects. Not a single part of me was clean. Even the personal accomplishments I prized—my published writing, superb academic record, and respect from my professors—were as filthy rags before the holiness of God, the standard by which the human race must be judged.

Because of my sin, I would surely die. There was only One who could cure this sickness, if I would only reach out to touch his robe.

After months of conflicting feelings about God and salvation and false images of Jesus from my childhood, I finally did.

Several months later, the Lord led me to a doctor who could cure my disease. But even if it had been his will for me to experience *dermatographia* for the rest of my life, he would have still been my comfort. He would have provided for me. He would have been all I needed, just as he is now.

I had to learn to rely on him in sickness so I could know he is just as faithful in trying conditions as he is when I am well. This is what allows me to be fully present in the story of the woman with the issue of blood—the knowledge that no circumstances can separate me from the love of God, which is in Christ Jesus, my Lord.[2]

Someday, just like this woman's, my faith will become sight. I will see his loving gaze and hear his voice speaking my name. And though I have not seen him yet, I know these will be far more refreshing than the physical cure and relief he brought me by his grace.

Your faith has made you well; go in peace.

---

2   Romans 8:38-39 KJV

SEE, HERE IS WATER

I

I have always wondered about the Ethiopian eunuch, the man the apostle Philip encountered in the desert after leaving Samaria. The one who was reading Isaiah 53 in his carriage and asked Philip about whom the author was speaking—this man who was *pierced for our transgressions and crushed for our iniquities.*[1] Philip's proclamation of the gospel through Isaiah's prophetic writings led this man to believe in Christ.

The historical context of Acts 8 tells us a lot about the eunuch. Though I long imagined him as a servant, he was the royal treasurer for the Queen of Ethiopia—an elected official. He would have been traveling in a comfortable, covered transport with servants of his own.

If we miss this fact, we miss a significant part of the story. The conversion of a court official would have been an extremely big deal. Historians report that the early church in Ethiopia grew quickly and thrived for many years because of the eunuch's initial act of faith.

---

1   Isa. 53:5 NIV

Philip had just left ecstatic crowds in the city of Samaria, and after having seen perhaps hundreds of people be saved, he may have wondered why the Holy Spirit would lead him into the middle of nowhere with seemingly no people in sight. But the Lord had one person in mind, someone powerful who would receive the message of salvation and then carry it into another country.

But these facts aren't all that interest me. What I'm most curious about is the water.

In the passage, the two men are traveling on the road discussing the scriptures when the eunuch abruptly cries out, "See, here is water! What prevents me from being baptized?"[2] What was the water? Considering that this all happened in a Middle Eastern desert, there couldn't have been much of it, perhaps barely enough for him to be fully immersed. There were no major bodies of water as described in the Gospels—no River of Jordan or Sea of Galilee. The water may have only a small pond muddied with wet sand and dirt. Yet, he so desired to be baptized that it was enough indeed.

I imagine Philip lowering the eunuch into the murky water, then raising him up, his body coated in filth and mud. Meanwhile, the royal attendants, who have become unwitting witnesses, watch, baffled. They have no idea what's just happened.

II

When I was six, my parents and I went on a beach vacation. I'd never seen the ocean before, and I stood on the sand, spellbound, gazing out at the surging, gray waves. There is a photograph of me from this trip sitting on the beach, proudly displaying a sandcastle I'd decorated with dribbles of wet sand.

I waded into the ocean, my feet submerged first, then my knees, until finally I was up to my waist. Through trial and error, I discovered the waves' rhythm and how to jump at the right moment to be carried upward and swim with the tide. I was gleefully floating along when a large wave took me by force and body-slammed me,

2   Acts 8:36 ESV

dragging me underwater. My legs dug into a rough layer of sand, and I struggled to pull my head above water until the wave finally spit me out, breathless, on the beach.

It was years before I could play in the ocean without fear.

III

In "The River," my favorite story by Flannery O'Connor, a neglected child, Harry Ashfield, goes for a day out with a babysitter, an old woman named Mrs. Connin. Harry's parents are rich society folks from the city who spend too much time partying with friends, which makes their child a liability. When Mrs. Connin arrives to pick Harry up, his mother is hung over and his father is so eager to shoo him out the door that Harry's arm isn't fully secured in his coat.

Mrs. Connin takes Harry into the country to a faith healing at a river. The preacher's message hinges mostly on the fanciful and miraculous, drawing heckling from a town cynic on the banks. But when Mrs. Connin takes Harry into the river to meet the preacher and be baptized, Harry instinctively knows that things will be different from now on. The preacher tells him about Jesus and the Kingdom of Heaven as he immerses him, and for the first time, Harry feels hope instead of the despair of his daily life. He feels a new sense of worth, knowing that rather than being cast aside as insignificant, he at last matters to someone. And that someone happens to be the King himself.

Harry arrives home later that night to discover one of his parents' parties in progress, and his mother immediately sends him to bed. The next morning, he wanders through the now-silent apartment, scrabbling together a breakfast of flat soda pop and crackers with anchovy paste. The emptiness of his life, which he had previously tolerated, is now unbearable. He realizes he has only one course of action: to return to the river and seek the Kingdom of God for himself.

Alone, Harry travels the same route he and Mrs. Connin took the day before. When he reaches the river, he plunges himself into the dirty water again and again until the current finally catches hold of him and sweeps him away. The world has nothing for him.

IV

I was not eager to be baptized. Though I was saved at age twenty-two, the memory of that day at the ocean was too much with me. I could immerse myself under the waters of a lake or a pool or even a bathtub. But to have someone else do it meant surrendering control, being vulnerable in the manner I was unwittingly thrust into all those years ago.

I see now, of course, that this is the whole point.

Three years after my conversion, I was finally compelled to be baptized. I understood that it was the example Christ set for us, one that the Apostles and the early converts, including the Ethiopian eunuch, obeyed. However, I faced a problem: I did not belong to a local church, and there was no congregation where I lived that I felt comfortable visiting.

Going to church terrified me—given my negative childhood experiences with religion, which were coated in condemnation and fear, I was stunned that I had even been saved at all, and I didn't want to risk being talked out of it. When I shared my desire to be baptized with a friend who had been discipling me since my conversion, he generously offered to come visit and baptize me himself.

I met him at the hotel where he was staying, and we went down to the pool. It was smaller than most hotel pools I'd been to, and harsh institutional lights beamed from the ceiling. The floor was covered in tiny rocks spackled together, and the November snow clouded the windows. We entered the water, which was mercifully warm. A family was hanging out in the shallow end, and my friend informed them that I was getting baptized as a believer in Jesus Christ and asked if they would serve as witnesses. They looked at each other and shrugged, seeming confused. Perhaps they wondered if this was okay, if baptism could really happen in a pool and not at a golden altar.

The family gathered near us as my friend and I took our places in the water. I affirmed that I believed in Jesus Christ, the Lord, the Messiah, the only begotten Son of God, that *I have been crucified with Christ, and I no longer live, but Christ lives in me.*[3] Before I went underwater, I asked if I could hold my nose. My friend laughed.

I was plunged downward. Chlorine flooded my eyes as I felt the weight of the water against me. But there was no gasping for air, no murky sea water clogging my lungs, no fear that I would never emerge. I did not fear this now, and when I finally rose upward, the lights above blinding and grating in my eyes, I knew I was safely on the shore.

---

3   Gal. 2:20 BSB

A LESSON FROM JAVERT

My husband and I met at a small church that held services in an elementary school gym. I was sitting in the back row of folding chairs because I had to leave early for my Sunday afternoon retail shift, and he was arriving late because his truck broke down. We spoke for thirty seconds, which was just enough time to exchange names and occupations. It was also just enough time to know that we would become important to each other.

Our relationship, which deepened over the next several months, revolved around life at our church. We took joy in serving together at community events, setting up the gym for the weekly services, and greeting people at the entrance on Sunday mornings. Outside of church, we studied the Bible, prayed, and talked about our passions. I loved writing and wanted to publish a novel. He was a machinist and liked working on old Dodge trucks.

We were close with our pastor, who was delighted that we had found each other in his congregation. He was also the first church leader my husband, who grew up as a believer, had ever connected with spiritually. The pastor was warm and friendly, with infectious energy, and he taught the Bible in a way that left us feeling encouraged and uplifted. Although this was the first church I'd ever been a part of since becoming a Christian, I found him relatable and easy to talk to, the opposite of the cold, harsh church leader I'd expected to meet when I came to my first service.

That Easter, my husband and I got engaged. A few months later, we were married in a small ceremony in a local park, with our pastor officiating. There is a picture of us standing with him under the eaves of the small wooden bridge that served as our altar, my husband and I looking at him with awkward, excited smiles. He had just made some joke neither of us expected.

Several months later, we learned that he was being sent out by our congregation to plant a new church in the same community we'd moved to after our wedding. This was an obvious draw since the church we were currently attending was almost a half hour away. More significantly, the prospect of ministering at home seemed like an ideal opportunity to serve God, and it seemed like a foregone conclusion that we would join the core team.

These motives were sincere, but in hindsight, I realize that we were also afraid of leaving our pastor. We trusted him, which was vital for switching churches. Going to church had been a massive step for me, since religious people had harmed me in the past. The idea of starting over with another pastor seemed overwhelming. Moreover, he and my husband had developed a friendship that my husband wasn't willing to abandon.

As more people joined us, we started to find our footing in the community. We held public Bible studies and outreaches at local festivals, where we handed out water bottles and did face painting for kids. My husband started playing guitar in the worship team, and I soon joined him on vocals. In the evenings after our events, we hung out at different people's houses for barbecues and bonfires, singing and discussing the Bible under the starry night sky.

Eventually, we got a permanent meeting space and started holding regular services. Gradually, more people learned about our congregation and began coming on Sundays. The more God opened doors for us, the more we were convinced that something special was happening, that we were making an impact in a place where the soil was hard.

I grew up listening to show tunes with my mom. One of my favorites was *Les Misérables*. Although I loved the music, I found the story difficult to follow. Even after seeing it performed, I struggled to understand its complex timeline and the connections between its many characters. Nevertheless, the songs seared into my memory, and although I didn't know what the show was about, I still knew all the words to "Master of the House" and "One Day More."

The first winter of our church plant's existence, the film adaptation of *Les Misérables* was released in theaters. My family went to see it the day after Christmas, and it was while watching Hugh Jackman and Anne Hathaway portray the characters of Jean Valjean and Fantine with heart-wrenching devastation and authenticity that I finally understood what the story was about. Moreover, because I was now a Christian, I grasped the more profound truth that had haunted the music since I first heard it.

The emotional core of the story is Jean Valjean's conversion to Christianity. Branded a criminal after his release from prison, Valjean is caught stealing silverware from a priest, who chooses to show him mercy rather than having him arrested for his offense. Shaken by this act of grace, Valjean dedicates his life to God and faithfully performs one act of self-sacrifice after another for the next twenty years. His compassion for the weak and helpless creates a ripple effect that rescues and transforms the people around him until he dies and, at last, receives his reward.

For weeks after seeing the movie, these themes, along with the story and music, ran through my mind. The lyrics I'd known my whole life now took on new meaning. I read the novel for the first time, delighting in its expansive narrative and how it widened the characters' backstories. I was also compelled to study the score and uncover its many biblical allusions. I was particularly drawn to the finale of "Do You Hear the People Sing?", which directly references Isaiah 2:4 (ESV):

> He shall judge between the nations,
>   and shall decide disputes for many peoples;
> and they shall beat their swords into plowshares,
>   and their spears into pruning hooks;
> nation shall not lift up sword against nation,
>   neither shall they learn war anymore.

Of course, this passage ultimately foretells the perfect rule of Christ in his coming kingdom. Yet, the implications of the ending of *Les Misérables*, where Valjean is joyously reunited in heaven with the characters who have preceded him in death, brought to life the glorious future of Jesus's followers in a way I'd never comprehended. All believers will one day stand before Christ and see the fruits of their lives displayed. There will be a reunion of all the saints, past, present, and future. More significantly, when the King himself returns, suffering, death, sickness, and violence—all things that devastate the lives of the characters in *Les Misérables*—will cease to exist.

I shared my review of the movie with people at the church plant, discussed my thoughts on the book with a couple of attendees who were familiar with it, and made many general references to the biblical themes I'd been driven to explore and their place in the narrative. I'd always seen art as a source of comfort, but once I believed in Christ, I discovered that it was complementary to my faith, not separate from it. I understood that most stories don't simply stand on their own but point to God's greater story of redemption and hope, and I wanted to share that with believers I knew.

This is the beauty of art for Christians: it can reframe spiritual realities and help us see God's word with new eyes.

That's why what happened next hit me so hard.

We'd just gotten home from church one night, and I was telling my husband about a recent discovery from my *Les Misérables* rabbit hole. He suddenly grew quiet and said we needed to talk. We sat on the edge of the bed, and he told me that our pastor had approached him that night with concern that I was giving myself over to entertainment and worldliness. I constantly talked about some book or movie rather than what I was studying in scripture. There had been many instances of this, but *Les Misérables* was the latest, and many people were suspecting me of worshiping idols. Some were even starting to ask questions about whether I was saved.

I stared at him in disbelief. I felt off-balance, as if the room were tilting around me. No one had ever told me anything was wrong with my passion for stories. More significantly, no one had ever insinuated that it meant I wasn't a Christian.

I waited for him to tell me that he understood that our pastor was wrong. He only shrugged and said that I *did* talk about movies a lot.

The next time we went to church, I felt anxious and ashamed, heavy with the weight of betrayal. When I saw our pastor inside the sanctuary, he gave me a look of warning that seemed to underscore the message he knew had been delivered.

Looking back, I empathize with my husband. Our church had begun to draw people from more legalistic religious backgrounds and to swing in a direction that favored a more authoritative leadership style. It would have been easy for him to panic at the possibility of being rejected by a pastor we'd been close to for so long or to worry about creating conflict within the church plant. I imagine most of us would react the same way.

While my pastor's position was hurtful, I can also understand part of it. If someone wasn't familiar with how I process art through a lens of faith, it would be easy for them to question where my true affections lay. After all, even if we have the best intentions, art can easily become an idol. The Old Testament is full of stories describing how man-made things, even those made for God's glory, can become objects of counterfeit worship. The bronze serpent Moses crafted was originally intended to be an instrument of God's glory, as all who looked upon it were healed from the plague of snakes. Yet, by the time of King Hezekiah's reign, people had begun to "make offerings to it"[1], leading Hezekiah to destroy the serpent in order to prevent further idolatry.

It is crucial for us to examine ourselves so we do not mistake the shadows that come through the arts for the substance that is Christ.

Nonetheless, our sovereign God's power can never be diminished or underestimated. He is able to use anything to draw people to himself and teach those who love him about his character. When properly viewed through the lens of his Word, the arts can become a tool for God to proclaim his glory.

Christian rap artist and author Sho Baraka has said that in order for healing to happen, "there has to be truth telling."[2] Though he says this in terms of handling interpersonal conflicts biblically, his words also apply to the ways Christians tell their stories to each other.

When we share the things that influence our faith—even unorthodox things such as movies—we tell the truth about how the Lord is working out our salvation. However, we only learn about how God can use the arts in sanctification through loving fellowship within the body, where iron sharpens iron as we work to understand each other without making assumptions about the state of a person's soul. When these assumptions are made, legalism takes root, and the very experiences that have drawn people to Christ can lead to rejection and alienation.

The need to understand each other's stories without judgment makes me think of Javert, the ruthless police officer who spends years chasing Jean Valjean. A friend once told me that during the intermission of a performance of *Les Misérables* that she attended, she overheard a woman call Javert "a despicable person." I don't see him this way. While it's true that his actions are self-righteous and cruel, Javert is not villainous. He is simply so zealous to enforce the

---

1   2 Kings 18:4 ESV

2   Sho Baraka, "Shaping the World with Stories" (Hutchmoot: Homebound, October 8, 2021).

law that he leaves no room for mercy and cannot grasp the damage he does to the less fortunate.

Meanwhile, Valjean, a criminal and a thief, unconditionally rescues the vulnerable at his own expense—including Javert. When presented with the opportunity to kill Javert, which would liberate him from a life on the run, Valjean instead chooses to spare Javert's life.

We, too, have the opportunity to do this for each other—to show mercy, no matter how others might respond to the stories we tell.

It's painful to recall that conversation with my husband, that first moment I realized I might not be accepted in the culture that was evolving within our church plant. But then I remember Baraka's words: healing happens when the truth is told. When we tell the truth with bitterness and the intent to shame, we lie about who Christ made us to be. When we do so in love, we shape our most painful stories into beauty.

I understand this now. But back then, the seeds of confusion about my identity in Christ had been planted, and the consequences were deadly.

After all this happened, I stopped talking with anyone at church about *Les Misérables*, or any art, for that matter. I tried only to speak if what I had to say was "safe." I became terrified of rejection, of ruining the church plant, of causing division, or of bringing shame upon my husband.

But alone in the car, I'd blast the final chorus of "Do You Hear the People Sing?" I let the meaning of the lyrics wash over me, reveling in the freedom that awaits us, the beating of the plowshares and the breaking of chains, while those words of rebuke haunted the corners of the melody.

SHE WILL BE SAVED THROUGH CHILDBEARING

We are having a baby dedication at church. Not we as in my husband and I, but we, the church congregation. We sit in rows of padded folding chairs, everyone watching with suppressed excitement as the mother and father come forward. They are not much older than twenty, and this is their first child.

The father holds the baby against his shoulder. She is tiny, swaddled, and maybe a month old. From my vantage point at the back of the room, she looks like a tightly folded sheet ready to be placed on a closet shelf. The people around us ooh and ahh as the father hands the baby to her mother. She looks down at the child in her arms, whispers something, and kisses her cheek.

This act is foreign to me.

The pastor begins the ceremony by reading from Psalms: *Like arrows in the hand of a warrior are the children of one's youth. Blessed is the man who fills his quiver with them!*[1]

Everyone nods in solemn affirmation.

They respond to the traditional congregational questions: *Will*

---

[1] Ps. 127:4-5 ESV

you support this couple as they raise their child? Will you do whatever is necessary to help them in this walk?

We will. We will.

After the service, cookies, coffee, and punch are served. The children play and yell at each other and run around until one of the older women commands them to stop. She smiles quietly and returns to a group of other women gathered in front of the coffee pot.

Such a beautiful ceremony. Beautiful family. Beautiful baby.

I sit in a chair against the wall and munch on a dry peanut butter cookie. The women's conversation blends together, their words weaving like threads into a misshapen garment.

And then, one phrase jumps out and holds me at knifepoint.

After all, motherhood is a woman's highest, holiest calling.

I feel like I'm going to puke.

As if somehow aware of this, one of the women suddenly says hello to me. She asks how I'm doing in a bumbling, awkward manner as if she means to draw attention to me in particular. I mutter some response or excuse and then go to the back of the sanctuary.

The thing is, I can't have children. My brain is broken, hormones and neurotransmitters battling for control. I need medication to keep all the electrical circuits connected and to direct the current where it's needed. Without it, I lose my focus, unable to sleep or work and crying without knowing why. This same medication, which has probably saved my life, also prevents me from getting pregnant.

But people here don't see that. They see it as a failure to trust in God, or perhaps to even be saved at all.

Nevertheless, I have to choose between being a mother and being a functional human being.

What's more, even if I did have children, I'm not sure I could handle it.

I force down the rest of the dry cookie and wipe the crumbs on the thighs of my jeans. The words *highest, holiest calling* ring in my ears like a fire siren. I take a deep breath and swallow; breathe and swallow again.

My husband comes over and asks if I'm okay. For a moment, I want to tell him what I heard. But there's no point in digging into it now. I tell myself that I must go back. They will wonder. They already wonder too much.

So, I follow him back to where everyone else is gathered, and as I walk past the group of women, I wonder: if motherhood is a woman's highest, holiest calling, is there any blessing left for a man beyond a quiver full of arrows?

Why I Dyed My Hair Purple

It all started one Sunday morning in March during that awkward time after a church service ends. Outside the sanctuary, everyone was milling around, chit-chatting. I stood next to the coffee pot, alone in the midst of the cliques around me, the blurred hum of their conversation echoing through the room.

As usual, I had nothing to say. Sunday morning banter came so easily to everyone else—the women especially. They slipped into such an easy routine around each other, talking about their children, husbands, and sewing projects.

I had no children, the best I could do with a needle and thread was fix a button, and cooking was a means of survival for me, not a joy. Sometimes, out of desperation, I would try to interject and talk about what was happening in the college classes I taught or a novel I was reading, or a story I'd just submitted for publication. But everything I could offer as polite conversation was met with a quiet *Oh, that's nice* or a stilted change in subject.

None of them seemed to know what to say around me, and I couldn't do much better. Sometimes, I wondered if their inability to connect with me was intentional. If they didn't take the time to listen, they could continue to live with the illusion that I was more like them.

That morning, the pastor approached one of the chatty groups of moms as they talked about their daughters. "Mine just dyed her hair," I overheard him say. "I keep telling her, 'If God wanted you to have pink hair, he would have made you that way.'" They laughed, but I could tell there was a part of each of them that believed this.

The following Saturday, I decided to chop off my shoulder-length brown hair and dye it purple.

I walked up to the counter of my local salon and made my request to the stylist.

"Hon, you sure you want to do that?" she said, almost as if she knew my situation.

"*Oh yeah.*"

She put me in one of those spinning chairs and mixed the dye, a thick, white-ish violet substance that smelled like turpentine, then applied it to my hair, shaping it tightly around my head. She set a timer for thirty minutes, then left me alone in front of the mirror. I looked like Norma Desmond at the end of *Sunset Boulevard*, descending the staircase after her collapse into madness.

When the timer went off, the stylist rinsed out the dye and cut my hair so it was angled in a sharp bob along my jawbone. Strands of it fell to the floor around me as the scissors snapped around my ears. She blow-dried my hair, then turned the chair around to reveal the results: a harsher, more aggressive version of myself.

Not content to stop there, I swung by J.C. Penney's to check out their current sale and left with a black leather jacket that I got for sixty percent off. I drove home blasting Lady Gaga's "Hair" out the open windows, the air thick with the lingering scent of dye as she sang about how she, too, had *enough*.

The next morning, I walked into church with my chopped-off purple hair and leather jacket. I wore mauve lipstick, and my eyes were done up with sandy-gold eyeshadow and dark brown eyeliner. "What on God's good earth have you done to yourself?" a woman asked, with a scandalized look on her face.

I shrugged. "I got bored."

I could sense people's eyes on me as I walked through the church. I knew it was likely that someone, the pastor or perhaps one of the elders, would pull my husband aside and ask why he couldn't control his wife. But I didn't care. It was exhilarating to be seen as someone other than the clean-cut, quiet woman they wanted to believe I was, a woman who didn't exist, who never had.

I have a picture from my purple hair era that my husband snapped on his phone during church. The drum set on the stage is in the background, so I was probably getting ready to sing with the worship team, which I did mostly because this was a congregation where you didn't say, "No." My slanted smile shows I'm clearly trying to look like Patti Smith or Neko Case or another one of those edgy rock chicks I liked. But instead of their strong, confident appearances, I just come across as sad. There is a vacant expression in my eyes. I'm wearing metallic blue lipstick and thick, black eyeliner. I look like I am imprisoned inside myself.

I'm not saying that all people who dye their hair are crying out for help. For many, it is a true expression of their individualism and creativity, and I'm sure that's what I wanted to believe about my own transformation. I know now, though, that I was crying out to be seen. When I tried to tell my story, share the things I loved, and communicate what it was like for me to walk with Jesus, no one paid attention. As a result, I was forced to do something more drastic.

Ironically, this was the approach that my favorite author, Flannery O'Connor, took to her writing. She famously explained that because she was writing primarily for unbelievers, she had to use grotesque and shocking means to communicate her message of grace. This is why her stories are populated with serial killers, false prophets, swindlers, and religious hypocrites. Tamer, more conventional Christian stories would never have grabbed the attention of the people who most needed her work. Readers had to have their senses overloaded with the unexpected so they could grasp the truths her stories communicated.

I think I was doing the same thing. If no one would listen, I needed to make sure they couldn't look away.

Over the years, I've told this story to numerous artists and writers who are Christians, and most have said my experience resonates with them. It's as if many churches have created a box that the Good Christian™ has to fit in, and if you don't, there is no place for you. Yet, this is precisely the opposite of what the apostle Paul writes about the church's identity: "For just as the body is one and has many members, and all the members of the body, though many, are one body, so it is with Christ. For in one Spirit we were all baptized into one body—Jews or Greeks, slaves or free—and all were made to drink of one Spirit."[1]

In a lecture given to writers of faith, novelist S.D. Smith quotes Reverend Chris Borah, saying that "we are not called to sameness, but to oneness."[2] The beauty of the oneness Christ desires of his bride is that our differences become secondary to the unity we have in the Holy Spirit. Moreover, our diverse experiences become gifts to the body as a whole, providing fresh ways of seeing the work the Lord is doing in his people's lives.

This reminds me of the Spotify playlist that my writing community creates every year for our summer retreat to Nashville. We all love beautiful, Christ-glorifying songs by Andrew Peterson, Sandra McCracken, Keith and Kristyn Getty, and many others. But when you hit shuffle, you'll also hear a selection of show tunes, metal, classical, '90s country, and fusion jazz. In the same way, believers are a diverse mix of backgrounds, nationalities, talents, and life experiences brought together by the One who, for his glory, has made us alive to be members of his body.

Today, I've grown my hair out, and it has returned to its natural shade of light brown. But sometimes, I look at selfies I took

---

1   1 Cor. 12:12-13 ESV

2   S.D. Smith, Lecture from HopeWords 2024 (Bluefield, WV, April 13, 2024).

during my purple hair era and feel a strange incongruity of emotions. I know I was crying out for someone to see me, to recognize how lonely and desperate for connection I was. It was an outward manifestation of my internal pain from having my identity and my faith picked apart like petals from a flower, an act of desperation to hold onto what I felt was slowly slipping away from me.

Now, I know I belong to Christ, and not just to him, but to the multitude who will someday cry with one voice, "Salvation belongs to our God who sits on the throne, and to the Lamb!"[3]

---

3   Rev. 7:10 ESV

AT LEAST THERE WERE BLUEBIRDS

When we first got married, my husband and I lived in a one-story, swayback ranch house with asbestos siding covered in peeling, red lead paint. The house was built in the '30s and then demolished and rebuilt twenty years later, leaving the foundation uneven with an unnatural rise in the floor. The house had been on the market for three years when we bought it two months before our wedding, but we never asked why. This young, newly-engaged couple was taken for suckers.

The house was built on a three-and-a-half-acre plot of land on a hill overlooking a small pond and a creek. Two enormous trees—one oak, one walnut—were stationed like sentinels at either end of the property. After we moved in, it was clear that we had work to do on the house. Yet, we still began to dream about our future in our new home. We imagined picnics under the tree, summer Bible studies by the creek for the children at the church we were helping to plant, and an enormous garden that would blanket every inch of the land.

But gardens cost money and time, and the trains that barreled down the railroad tracks across the street drowned out any conversation, leaving no room for the words of children. Soon, other issues began to emerge. The minerals that poured into the well made it the hardest water in the whole state, and within two months of moving in, my hair had turned brittle, forcing me to shower at the gym. Even then, orange rust stains would cover the bathtub, which I had to scour with a corrosive lime mixture until my shoulders ached and my hands grew sticky with sweat inside my vinyl gloves.

Meanwhile, life at the church plant had grown demanding and twisted. At every turn, I was doing something wrong. I was branded "too liberal" for seeing the value of stories that portrayed the reality of sin and death in this fallen world. I didn't check the boxes of being a good Christian woman—I was married without children, failing to create new soldiers for the Kingdom, and appeared to be more interested in my creative ambitions and career than doing the *real* work of starting a family. I had severe mental health issues, and, according to my congregation, I was sinning by seeking medical treatment instead of repenting of whatever secret sin was probably causing the problem.

But the worst part of our remote life was the loneliness. It seemed to stretch for miles, leaving me aching and empty. No neighbors. No one nearby. Even when we went into town, especially to church, there was the pain of unbelonging and the feeling that no one cared, not even the people who were supposed to. Our property was so remote that satellite internet was our only available option, and my online connections had to be reserved for my work-at-home job, with no frivolous uses allowed. The winters were bitterly cold, for there was no electric heat, and we could not consistently afford propane.

Finally, a conflict unfolded within our church that left us no choice but to leave. Once this crucial tie to the community was cut, living on the property became unsustainable. We decided that the best option was to renovate the house and sell it, but this, too, presented problems. Much of the structure was worn beyond repair, to the point of being dangerous. When my husband opened the electrical box to begin rewiring the house, the ancient wires disintegrated in his hands. He spent years making the house livable just so we could get rid of it.

One spring afternoon, I was sitting on the back of my husband's pickup truck reading when I saw a streak of blue and orange moving in a small tree near the house. A bluebird was perched on one of the limbs, fluffing its feathers. Then another bluebird landed next to it, and then another.

I put down my book and watched them, studying their bright feathers, the colors like delicately blended dabs of an artist's paints. I'd seen bluebirds before, but only in passing. That afternoon, there were three, and they stayed for several minutes, bright and lively against the budding leaves, giving me the rare chance to observe their beauty.

Nine years after we moved in, in the middle of winter, we finished the renovations and finally sold the house. It was snowing when we backed down the long driveway for the last time.

We live in a small town now, in a development with sidewalks and neighbors. Just three blocks away is our church, and I frequently see friends as I ride my bike through the streets. Our house is warm and comfortable with consistent heat, clean water, and plenty of internet. I am thankful for these provisions. In our backyard are flocks of robins, the occasional cardinal, and a family of rabbits that burrows their babies every spring.

But there are no bluebirds—and I often wish there were. Because I last saw them in a time of isolation and depression, they remind me of God's faithfulness—how even when there seems to be no hope, the work of his hands cries out, reminding us to worship the One who ordains our days.

MIRACLE DRUG

U2 frontman Bono often tells the story of how he became a songwriter. It was his eighteenth birthday, and he was blasting the Ramones' "Glad to See You Go" in his family's living room. The band's high-energy punk sound captured the imagination of the Irish teenager, who had spent the last few years reeling from the sudden death of his mother and the distant relationship with his father and brother that followed.

But at last, Bono had discovered a way out of his personal prison: he was going to become a songwriter too. He already had a song idea, and though he hadn't put it down on paper yet, he knew it was destined to be the first record he would make with the band he'd recently formed with his three best friends. He would bring the song into being, and with it, the first glimpse of hope he'd experienced since his family was blown apart.[1]

There was a world beyond this anguish, and he was standing on its shores. The Ramones had made this possible. More than forty years later, Bono paid tribute to that moment in U2's "The Miracle (Of Joey Ramone)," to an artist whose music he calls "beautiful."

---

1   "Out of Control - 'Surrender: 40 Songs, One Story' by Bono." YouTube, May 10, 2022. https://www.youtube.com/watch?v=_B7Qt861IJI.

It might be hard for many people to see "Glad to See You Go"—or any of the Ramones catalog, for that matter—as beautiful. Their arrangements (if you want to call them that) are chaotic and harsh. The vocals are screamed rather than sung, and the lyrics are nearly impossible to understand. Yet, the Ramones, with all their rebellious bravado, reached out to a troubled teen who was still trying to comprehend his mother's death and how a way forward could even be possible. Their music gave him a passion for songwriting and a vision for a future he'd been too consumed with grief to imagine.

The music we most need always finds its way to us, guided by the hand of God.

In early 2017, my husband and I made a painful break with the church we'd helped to plant five years before. The hope and excitement we initially felt about creating something new had grown cold in the face of legalism and emotional abuse. We were imprisoned by the expectations of others, fearing what might happen if we chose to walk out like Paul and Silas did when the Holy Spirit opened the prison gates.

We were founding members, and we couldn't just *quit*. Instead, we got used to the manipulation, gaslighting, and control. We made excuses for this abuse and sublimated it until we finally realized, almost too late, that this was a matter of life and death, and we had to leave.

The next Sunday, we started attending a church where one of our friends went. My faith felt like it was on life support, and I didn't understand why I even wanted to go to church at all after everything that had happened. It felt counterintuitive, yet I knew that if I had any hope of recovering from the damage, I had to keep moving forward. Nonetheless, part of me still looked askance at Jesus, wondering if my faith would ever be the same again.

Around this time, my husband discovered U2. I had a brief affair with their landmark album, *The Joshua Tree*, in high school, but for some reason, my interest had stopped there, as if back then, I wasn't ready to truly experience their work. Now, as their albums entered our home one by one I dove into each of them, captivated by the Edge's stirring guitar solos and Bono's lyrics. Their songs are imbued with a passion for God and his creation, and the more I listened, the more I felt my forgotten knowledge and love for Christ, which had lain dormant and frozen for months, begin to wake up.

The beauty of U2 is that they rarely sing about their faith with directness. Instead, their songs are full of scriptural allusions and subtle turns of phrase that reinforce the deeper presence of Christianity in their music. They write modern-day psalms that explore spiritual struggle, lament, longing, and anger with agonizing honesty. Like the lyrics composed by King David, there is a beautiful tension in their work that mirrors the push and pull of assurance and doubt that comes with walking by faith. It is this tension that allows Bono to confess in one of their best-known songs, "I Still Haven't Found What I'm Looking For," that he is searching for meaning in this fallen world while also proclaiming his belief in its redemption through the coming King.

The song that captured my attention most was "Miracle Drug." It was inspired by a classmate from Bono's childhood, Christopher Nolan, who developed cerebral palsy after being deprived of oxygen at birth. Paralyzed, Nolan could neither communicate verbally nor in writing. Years later, though, his doctors discovered a drug that enabled him to move a single muscle in his neck, allowing him to learn to type using a special device and keyboard. Granted the use of language for the first time, Nolan experienced a flood of creativity as the thoughts that had been imprisoned in his mind finally found release. He eventually published a book of poetry, *Dam-Burst of Dreams*, and became a celebrated Irish author.[2]

Even without knowing Nolan's story, I felt this desperate catharsis and longing for self-expression the first time I heard "Miracle

---

2   "Christopher Nolan: Irish Author Who Overcame Cerebral Palsy to Win the Whitbread Prize at the Age of 21." *The Independent*, February 23, 2009.

Drug." Its atmospheric guitar riffs and driving rhythm section enveloped my scarred, hesitant soul in its four-minute world and held me there, whispering *it's okay, it's over now, you're safe*. Its treatise on beauty, love, and music seemed to be addressed directly to me at that moment, showing that my love of art mattered not just to my well-being but to God. Bono describes the beauty of watching someone hear music and seeing how the songs cause them to practically explode with joy.

Perhaps, I thought, this is how God sees me. The music, films, and stories that inspire me are not there by accident, but have been strategically placed in my path, each providing a way for me to learn something new about him, myself, and his world.

It was the purest, clearest message I'd heard since my captivity inside man-made religion. The music and words of U2 swung a door wide open, a blinding light broke through the darkness, and I walked out into it.

Music, of course, is not a replacement for God. It is not scripture, prayer, fellowship, or other disciplines that lead to growth in Christ. But it can be the threshold of these things, especially for people who are hurting from the wounds of false religion and feeling as if their faith has been shattered. God knows no genre distinctions, no barriers between the secular and sacred. He intimately knows the work of creators because he is *the* Creator. He delivers songs to the people who need them most, and not a moment too late or too soon.

Every good thing given and every perfect gift is from above, coming down from the Father of lights, with whom there is no variation or shifting shadow.[3]

---

3 James 1:17 ESV

Did You Know Jesus Can Breathe Underwater?

I have a young friend at church named Peter. He is six years old, big for his age, with a wide, excited smile and wild, curly hair. He is in my children's Sunday school class, where we act out Bible stories, draw pictures, and pray about test anxiety, bullies, pets, and family.

After class is over, Peter likes to come sit next to me during worship. One day, as the congregation was singing a hymn, he tugged on my sleeve, and I leaned down to hear what he had to say. He told me that because Jesus can breathe underwater, his cousin Sarah did a trust fall into a tub and came back up.

It took me a minute to realize that he was describing his cousin's baptism last summer. When I asked him if that was what he was talking about, he said yes. Then, he asked me what blaptize meant. The congregation kept on singing, the notes lofting all around us. I told Peter to ask me after the service ended, or better yet, to ask his grandfather, who had baptized her.

I keep thinking about what Peter said. I'm not sure about Jesus breathing underwater. He doesn't need to—after all, he made the water, and as God, he is omnipresent. Moreover, Jesus himself was baptized, setting an example that demonstrated submission to his Father.

Clearly, there are some theological dilemmas at work. But I think he got the rest of it right.

It is a fall. It requires trust. And though all of us without exception have fallen, by grace we are raised up.

NEAR MISSES

It's been one of the bad days. At work, I sat at my computer for seven hours spam testing emails and chatting with tech support, glancing at the clock and asking myself, as I often do these days, what it all means, why any of what I do even matters.

I'm so tired I can't stand it. So tired that I ache.

At four-thirty, I cash it in and go home early to get in a bike ride before meeting with my counselor at seven o'clock. I talk to a friend on the way home and make a dumb wisecrack that this whole COVID situation might just blow over the minute the election ends.

He doesn't get that I'm kidding. Instead of laughing, he tells me it will be another couple of years at least—*at least*—and the second wave isn't even here yet.

At home, I suit up in my bike clothes and put air in my tires, then head out on the road. It's windy and my legs are complaining, my bicycle crawling forward. A guy in a yellow pickup truck passes me and blares his horn. Meanwhile, "Exile" by Taylor Swift and Bon Iver plays through my AirPods, their voices and eerie piano chords blending over the landscape of farmland and the winding road up ahead.

As I get ready to cross the railroad tracks that cut through the road to the bike trail, I notice too late that the gates are closing for an approaching train. I swerve through them, the train in full view, then fly toward the trail. A guy stares at me from the trail parking lot in what is either awe or disgust at my stupidity.

I remember the words painted on a sign next to the train tracks where I grew up. *Maybe you can beat the train. Maybe you're dead wrong.*

I keep pedaling into the wind, feeling foolish and reckless. I shouldn't have done that. It would have been better just to take another route than risk my life.

But then I start thinking . . . what if I *had* gotten clipped by the train?

It would be over. No more wondering about how everything ends. No more fear that my loved ones will die or that I won't be able to handle the future none of us can predict. I know I shouldn't entertain this fantasy, but I'm too tired to fight against it. I imagine my carbon fiber bike crumbled like tin foil, the smear of my body on the tracks.

Before I can continue down this morbid rabbit hole, I reach the end of the trail. I down an entire bottle of water mixed with a grape electrolyte tablet, the fizzy tartness swirling on my tongue. My energy has piqued a little, but I'm still so tired, and now I need to make it home, and I'm starting to think this whole ride was a mistake. With no other choice, I get back on my bike and turn around.

I've gone about half a mile when a flash of tan and white sweeps in front of me—a large doe bounding across the bike trail. Stunned by my presence, she comes to a sudden halt. I stop pedaling and let myself naturally slow down, creeping ahead so as not to scare her away.

She pauses, glances at me, and flicks her tail before darting off the trail, and I watch her disappear into the trees. I am about to start moving again when two fawns dash out of the bushes, running together like two toddlers, crying out, *wait for me, wait for me.*

I dig into the pedals and push myself forward. There's still life here.

SUNLIGHT

Last winter pierced me like a cold steel blade. It wasn't just the external—the whiplash of midwestern wind, the shortened, early-dark days, the sky so thick and gray that it was impossible to imagine the sun. It was more about the internal, the way its chilled fingers reached deep inside me, running over the curves of my brain and distorting the things inside it that were already broken.

I felt the heaviness every day upon waking. Outside, the naked branches smacked each other with an icy crackle, and simply moving my body seemed to take all my strength. Downstairs, I made coffee, relying on its rich scent to bring me to life. I read my Bible; I opened up my prayer journal and asked the Lord, as I did every day, to bring me relief from this darkness, to restore my energy and sense of hope. The pressure of pen on paper, the smooth ink drying on the page, and the words in my mind taking shape before me made my prayers easier for me to grasp, connecting me in a more tangible way with the frustration and sadness I seemed entangled in.

People think depression is just about feeling sad, but for me, it runs deeper than that. My body ached everywhere in a way I couldn't pinpoint. I did my best to drag myself through my day—client calls, writing, reading, family obligations—but it never felt like enough. I felt imprisoned doubly, not just inside winter, but inside my own body, inside my expectations of what I believed I should be able to do, but physically could not. At the end of the day, I desired only sleep, to be separated from the world for a while, to allow myself to rest, until the sky lightened through the oppressive layer of clouds, and it all began again.

I yearned for sun, the wet smell of spring, the sturdiness of pavement beneath my bicycle wheels, and the small animals and rush of leaves on my favorite trail. I continued to pray. For the clouds to part, just for a moment, so I could see the sun. For my increased dose of Lexapro to even out the weight inside my head. For just one normal day, where I could feel like myself and actually enjoy the tasks ahead of me.

It didn't come, at least not wholly. But there was grace.

The medication change worked. I listened to vinyl records, the music filling me with something warm and tactile. I met up with friends at a writing conference out of state and felt the joy of true creative fellowship. I discovered chai tea with honey and a dash of almond milk and took a class on Zoom about Narnia and the *Dawn Treader's* own tempestuous, endless voyage.

And then, one day in March, I awoke to a clear, cloudless sky. I stepped outside to feel a warm breeze and a familiar trace of sun. I aired up my bike tires, filled my water bottles, put in my earbuds, and carried my bike outside.

On the road, the wind was at my back. I headed onto a country road that leads to the familiar trail, where the branches were still bare, but hints of buds emerged, signs of things waking up. I dug into the pedals and felt my legs tighten and release with each stroke, my speed building, the wheels bounding over the rise and fall of the pavement, the sun rays warming the sleeves of my riding jersey. The groundhogs and squirrels crept from their hibernation and darted down the edges of the trail. The air smells different when the world is coming to life again, and that scent was all around me, a deep, earthy freshness that smelled like hope.

After a long winter filled with the burdens of illness and the bitter chill, nothing ever made me feel so healed, so free.

THE VIRTUOUS WOMAN

I f we look beyond the familiar words of scripture and the distance of the centuries, we can see it: the city of Bethlehem in an uproar, the hustle and bustle near the city gates rising above its usual intensity. A rush of whispers spreads through the gathering crowd as people strain to see the woman approaching.

"Is that her?"

"It has to be. Look at her eyes. I'd know them anywhere."

"But she looks so . . . old. So frail. Is it really *Naomi*?"

Weak and weary from her long journey from Moab, Naomi limps into their midst. She is a wisp of the strong, joyful woman who left years ago with her family to find food during the famine. Her husband and sons, who surely would be grown by now, are disturbingly absent.

It's then that the people notice something else. A young woman they've never seen before is following close behind her. A Moabite woman. There is a tinge of fear in her eyes, yet she steels herself with duty and determination.

The crowd gathers around these two women, eager to hear what's happened. Little by little, the story comes out in small, painful scraps.

Naomi's husband, Elimelech, is dead. Worse still, Mahlon and Chilion, who were just boys when they left home, are dead as well.

The women gasp. Some are shattered by the death of the sons, while others are merely shocked by the scandalous news about their Moabite wives—women of a nation born from incest.

But there's more. The Moabite girl accompanying Naomi is Mahlon's widow. She has forsaken her own people and chosen to bind herself to Naomi, to the Hebrew people, and to Yahweh, their God. Her name is Ruth.

"Why would she do *that*?" a woman whispers. "Give up her family and her home? With no possibility of Naomi bearing any more sons for her to marry?"

Naomi blinks as though she is about to cry, but no tears come. Her face is weathered and dry. She glances in the woman's direction with a cold, hollow stare. "Do not call me Naomi," she says. "Call me Mara, for the Lord has dealt very bitterly with me."

Meanwhile, Ruth watches from a short distance away, the emptiness growing inside her. Naomi forgets that she is grieving too, that the only way out of this is to lean on each other.

Even though it was awkward and uncomfortable, I went to the women's Bible study at the church plant. I was too afraid to not go; if I wasn't there, people would wonder why, and it would be yet another thing that I'd done wrong, another rule I'd broken. We met at different homes on a rotation and gathered in the living room with tea or coffee and our Bibles. The studies consisted of workbooks with full-page photos of flowers or home décor captioned with Jeremiah 29:11, Romans 8:28, and of course, Proverbs 31.

This group, and the church in general, viewed Proverbs 31 as a checklist for a good Christian woman. If you were married, you were expected to raise children who were well-behaved and faithful to the Lord. You needed to keep your house in order at all times.

You should set a good example in your community and never disgrace your husband. You were to be prepared for all situations, rise while it was still dark, never waste time being idle, and always conduct yourself with wisdom and strength. This and nothing less was what God expected of women.

To them, all this seemed obvious, even effortless. But whenever they discussed these requirements, I felt hopeless and embittered. I was not able to have children for reasons beyond my control. I was far from domestic, and we lived in a slipshod, old house that was impossible to keep clean. I was a fiction writer, which they saw as a waste of time since none of my work mentioned Jesus or featured characters experiencing dramatic conversions in the third act. Similarly, many things I loved, like the beautiful stories in books, films, and songs, were considered worthless and sinful no matter how greatly they enriched my soul and inspired my creativity.

And, considering all these failures, I was sure there was nothing positive my husband would have to say about me.

I believed that these instructions were indeed what God required of me, but I was not able to follow them. The more I tried, the more weary I became. Whoever the woman described in Proverbs 31 was, she was holier and more capable than I was, and there was no way that I could possibly measure up to her.

Throughout the Book of Ruth, Ruth is repeatedly referred to as "Ruth the Moabitess"[1] or "the Moabite woman."[2] This is the primary lens through which people judged her: an outcast and a foreigner, a poor stranger from a country with a sordid history.

Though Ruth knew she had done the right thing by sealing her commitment to Naomi, I can only imagine the shame she must have felt when people gossiped about her or looked at her with suspicion.

---

1   Ruth 1:22 LSB
2   Ruth 2:6 LSB

She was from the wrong side of the tracks. Her husband was dead, and she didn't seem to be making an effort to find another one. Instead, she worked all the time, gleaning the fields for wheat and barley to bring home to Naomi. While many looked upon her with admiration, there were surely those who didn't understand why she didn't just stay with her own people and move on with her life.

So often, believers—women in particular—cling to the corners of small places, afraid of being misunderstood or of their intentions being misjudged. When their lives do not fit into the boxes of others' expectations, it's easy for people to jump to conclusions about their character.

In reality, however, our actions—though seemingly unconventional—may nonetheless be glorifying to the Lord, for he is pleased with them.

Recently, my husband and I visited a different church congregation. During the service, the pastor announced that they would be starting a new study on the Book of Ruth. He began explaining the story's literary characteristics and the author's masterful storytelling ability. As a writer, I immediately perked up, drawn in as he laid the groundwork for the context of Ruth's journey in a language I thoroughly understood.

Later in the sermon, he told us to turn to Proverbs 31. Instantly, I felt my body seize up. Ever since we'd left the church plant years earlier, reading Proverbs 31 felt like being pricked with burning needles—a painful reminder of my inadequacies. As a result, the passage had gathered dust in my Bible for years, tainted by memories of other women's harsh words and unrealistic expectations.

My husband leaned over and whispered that I needed to give the pastor's message a chance. I nodded and took a deep breath.

To my surprise, he began to expound on the passage by pointing out the similarities between Ruth and the Proverbs 31 Woman.

The parallels are striking. The language Boaz uses in Ruth 3:11 to describe her is also used of the woman in Proverbs: virtuous, worthy, and diligent. But that's not all. Proverbs 31:23 moves beyond the traits of the excellent wife to paint a picture of her husband, who is known at the city gates and serves as a respected leader. This perfectly illustrates Boaz, the well-known farmer and businessman who stood at those same gates and called for witnesses to hear him declare Ruth to be his wife.

At that moment, the checklist for the Proverbs 31 woman that had left me so thoroughly beaten was torn in two. The woman of Proverbs 31 was no longer a nebulous entity. She now had a name and a face. Her excellence became not a burden for me to carry but a glorious picture of Ruth's life after her Kinsman-Redeemer rescued her and Naomi, not to mention her and Boaz's inclusion in the genealogy of the Messiah.

I have often heard that Ruth's story is a picture of the gospel. At great personal cost, Boaz redeemed Ruth and brought her into his household to be his bride, welcoming Naomi as well. This is what Christ has done for his church. By grace through faith, we are freed from the burden of not being good enough. We are saved through the price paid by the Lord Jesus Christ, our Redeemer. We are not our losses, our griefs, or the parts of our pasts that people would rather ignore. We belong to *him*.

I'd never considered this beautiful truth.

Like Ruth, I am redeemed.

I have a name.

I am virtuous, dignified, and priceless beyond rubies.

THE FELLOWSHIP OF KINDRED MINDS

A week after deciding to leave the church plant, my husband and I drove an hour to worship at a friend's congregation. We were still shaken by the climax of the subtle and not-so-subtle spiritual abuse that had been in the background since we'd joined the core team five years before. The increasing tension between my husband and the church leadership had finally come to an impasse, and we realized that we couldn't pretend everything was okay anymore.

We were overwhelmed with sadness and anger, but when our friend learned about our situation and invited us to come to the service, we agreed. We knew the best course of action was not to distance ourselves from church but to plunge forward. Sitting alone in our grief would only make things worse.

The church was at the far end of a small, rural town. The building was easily a hundred years old and towered over the main intersection. Its brick walls were chipped with age, and the steeple held an enormous bell. This was new for us, going to an actual church building. Our previous two congregations were both young, and the church plant had met at an eclectic assortment of public facilities, including a bowling alley and a funeral home.

We parked the car and went inside. I knew that since my husband had already filled our friend in on the situation, there would be no need for an awkward and painful explanation of why we were there. But I still felt sick as we headed for the entrance. After all, there would be other people there too. Strangers. It had been a long time since I'd attended church without having to justify every aspect of my life. I was out of explanations, and the act of giving them so often had left me drained and hopeless.

In the fellowship hall, coffee and an array of snacks were set up near the adjacent kitchen. People were sitting around talking at various tables. Our friend came up to welcome us. "We call this Coffee and Conversation," he explained, gesturing around the room. I frowned. Coffee sounded great. I wasn't sure about the conversation part.

I wandered over to the snack and drink area, persuaded by the promised coffee. A woman named Meg with bouncy, blonde hair was there with her two young children, who were begging her to let them have more donuts. She quietly told them they were done eating, then gave me an apologetic smile.

I looked Meg and her children up and down. At the church we'd come from, moms had only one motive: to convince me that something was wrong with me because I wasn't one of them.

She offered me a cup of coffee, served with French vanilla half-and-half. I stirred it with one of those red plastic sticks. We stood next to the table in silence. I kicked my shoe against the tiled floor.

"What is it that you do?" she finally asked.

I looked around the room. Everything was beige and brown— the floor, the cupboards, the walls. A giant map of the world with pins in the countries where the church was supporting missionaries hung on a bulletin board on the opposite wall. I felt like a hostage who had just been rescued; I was disoriented and hadn't yet realized I was finally safe.

"I'm a writer," I said hesitantly. "And I teach some college classes."

Her eyes widened with what seemed to be genuine interest. "That's *amazing*. What do you write?"

I looked down at the floor, picking at the skin at the edge of my thumbnail. I took a long sip of coffee, then answered, "Fiction. Literary, historical." I glanced at her pointedly. "I don't write Christian stuff."

And then I waited.

"Oh, neat," Meg said. "I love to read. Is any of your work online? Can you send me a link or something?"

"Sure . . ."

"Awesome. So, what about you and your husband? Do you guys have kids?"

"No." I took another silent sip of coffee and waited again. The voices of the women at our old church played faintly in my head like a scratched record. *Motherhood is a woman's highest, holiest calling.* I waited for the other shoe to drop. The accusations. The shame that always followed.

Instead, she breezed past my answer. "Okay, cool. Well, we're so glad you came today. There's Sunday school upstairs, but if you just want to hang out here and drink more coffee, that's fine too."

I raised my head. Yes, I would like more coffee, to talk, to enjoy this moment when I'd told someone who I was and not been pushed away.

It was the first time I realized I was going to be okay.

In eighth grade, I was cast in our class's production of Thornton Wilder's *Our Town.* I played Mrs. Gibbs, the mother of the play's hero, George. George's relationship with the town sweetheart, Emily Webb, is the story's emotional core. The play revolves around their lives in the close-knit community of Grover's Corners—their courtship, marriage, and Emily's eventual death.

I think I was the only girl who didn't want to play Emily. I was thrilled to be cast as Mrs. Gibbs, a devoted wife and mother who married too young to know what she was getting into, yet still reminisced about her wedding and early life with her husband.

In one scene, the ladies of Grover's Corners attend choir practice at the church. To prepare for this scene, the female cast members met in the auditorium before first period every day for a week to learn the song we would sing, an old hymn called "Blest Be the Tie That Binds." As the rest of the school bustled through the hallways to get to homeroom on time, we sat in a row of chairs next to the stage, rehearsing its simple words and lilting melody:

> *"Blest be the tie that binds*
> *Our hearts in Christian love*
> *The fellowship of kindred minds*
> *Is like to that above."*[1]

I was a little ticked off about having to sing about God in school. But like a true method actor, I chalked it up as a necessity for authentically playing my character. Plus, I liked the words *fellowship* and *kindred*; their archaic syllables made me think that if I knew what those things were, I might like them too.

Recently, I reread *Our Town* just for fun. It's a surreal experience reading a play you were in once—sensory details locked in your subconscious for years are released in a flood. I was hit all at once with the damp scent of the old school auditorium and the poking sensation of bobby pins against my scalp. As I read the dialogue between Mr. and Mrs. Gibbs on the day of George and Emily's wedding, I remembered how the boy who played my husband and I reveled in rehearsing the dialogue as a kind of middle-aged, flirtatious banter. The play's message of the passage of time for young people in a small town felt bittersweet and poignant for me twenty-five years after performing in it.

But reading the choir practice scene unnerved me in a way I didn't expect. After the women are dismissed, a few gather outside

---

1   Roeleveld, Lori Stanley. "'Blest Be the Tie That Binds': Hymn Lyrics, Author, and Meaning." Christianity.com, June 29, 2023. https://www.christianity.com/wiki/christian-life/blest-be-the-tie-that-binds.html.

the church to gossip about Simon Stimson, the music director. Simon is an alcoholic, and a couple of the women are outraged because they suspect he was drunk for practice. While two of their companions (including Mrs. Gibbs) encourage them to show mercy to Simon, who has struggled personally, the others flatly insist that he needs to be removed from his position at the church. Then, as quickly as the subject arises, it drops, as the women make bland remarks about how beautiful the flowers look in the moonlight.

I paused for a moment, thinking about Simon Stimson. We're never told what his specific difficulties are or what circumstances led to his drinking, but I don't think that's the point. What struck me for the first time was how chilling the exchange between the choir members is. These women, who moments ago were singing about the blessed ties between believers, are now berating Simon for his sins while overlooking his emotional pain. In the final act of the play, which takes place in the Grover's Corners graveyard, the audience learns that Simon eventually committed suicide.

So it was in Wilder's time. So it is today.

Sometimes, stories are the only way to reveal the most painful truths of the world around us, including our immediate circles. It's easy to become blind to these things, to make excuses for people, justify behavior, or even ignore them altogether. Accommodating manmade preferences takes precedence over obeying God's Word. When that happens, we forget the grace he has bestowed on us and the reality of our undeserved salvation.

And if all this is true—if stories are the means by which these realities are revealed—the church needs writers more than it can possibly imagine.

A couple of weeks later, we visited our friend's church again. We were encouraged by the kindness of the people we'd met, a stark contrast to the alienation and abuse we'd previously experienced.

Although we didn't know what the future held for us, we needed to remember what it was like to feel safe at church. We needed compassionate believers to help us heal from the toxic legalism that had kept us in bondage.

This time, we were there for their monthly communion service. At first, it was not much different from other communion practices we'd been a part of. The deacons came to the front of the sanctuary for the traditional readings of the Last Supper passages. We paused together to remember Christ's sacrifice and reflect on his death and resurrection. We took the bread and the cup together.

But then, everyone stood up and formed a circle around the church, joining hands with the people beside them. A kid sitting near me motioned for my husband and me to come stand with him. Standing near the front of the sanctuary, I took in the array of people before me—the ecstatic children, some with their parents, some across the room with friends; older men and women who had been attending services together since they were children, their faces aged with wisdom; a young girl in a homemade flared dress patterned with Disney characters; and a weathered, middle-aged lady wearing a flannel shirt, jeans, and work boots.

The church tradition was that everyone stood in a circle after taking communion, holding hands, and singing "Blest Be the Tie That Binds."

As the organist played the opening chords, it all came back to me in an instant—that damp smell of the old auditorium, the sound of our untrained girl-voices rising to the high ceiling, the pain of those bobby pins poking my scalp, the nerves of opening night. I sang out the lyrics on autopilot as if the show had just been performed yesterday.

When we sat down, my husband put his hand on my knee and leaned over. "How did you know that song?" he whispered.

It had been years since I'd even thought of that hymn, its lyrics rising from the corners of my mind the way the notes had risen up from the organ pipes. I thought of that long-ago choir scene and the strange words in my mouth turned sweet. I didn't understand them before, but the more I thought about it, the more I saw their significance.

Fellowship is bigger than a single church congregation. The same Holy Spirit creates an intimate connection among *all* those who belong to Christ. This is why our gifts are for the building up of his body; our special abilities strengthen our intimacy as well as our faith. But none of this can happen without first experiencing fellowship with the Father, for without him, we can do nothing.

Ever since I became a Christian, I've struggled with how my faith and gifts as a writer intertwine, or whether they do at all, and how they serve the community around me. For a long time, it was an exercise in extremes. At first, I avoided going to church for fear that my newfound love for Jesus would be picked apart until nothing remained. Later, I let the church nearly consume me, plagued by notions that I wasn't good enough and that my writing was a symptom of my problems and a waste of my potential to live for Christ.

But now, I see that it is all by God's design. If I truly am his workmanship, my talents and desires are here on purpose, to build up his people, to strengthen the bond we share. Not only that, but I am responsible for stewarding them well, in honesty and love. As Jesus said, those who are faithful over a little will be set over much.[2]

I am accountable to my Father for using my stories well, both the ones I invent and the ones he has given me to tell: about how, long before I submitted myself to him, his Spirit was hovering over the deep of my soul.

2 Matt 25:23 ESV

ACKNOWLEDGMENTS

To begin with, this book would not exist without Jonathan Rogers and the support, collaboration, and hospitality of The Habit. This community for writers of faith is something truly special. I thank each of the Habitués who gave me feedback and encouragement on this project, which has truly been a group effort. As JR likes to say, we have brought glory to The Habit Membership.

Thank you to my friends at the Rabbit Room for showing me that there are other people like me in the world who love Jesus and the beautiful creative expression of people made in his image. Our conversations have demonstrated to me that my experiences aren't unique and that courageously sharing them can bring comfort to others and healing to still-tender wounds.

To Samantha Cabrera, Madison Aichele, Allana Walker, Lara d'Entremont, Rosa Gilbert, and the rest of the Calla Press Publishing team—you have helped me transform this project into something even more beautiful than I imagined it could be. Thank you for catching my vision and bringing your creativity, insight, and skill to my publication journey. I am so incredibly thankful for this opportunity.

Thank you to the editors of *Solid Food Press, Agape Review, Kosmeo, Shenandoah, Winter Pages,* and *Clayjar Review,* in which versions of essays in this book previously appeared.

To Frank Ewert, S.D.G. Morgan, Kimberly Crislip Jarvis, Dr. Alan Trimble, Heinz and Jane Burchard, and Mark and Rhonda Rice—thank you for helping me ask the hard questions and showing me how to write about painful experiences while showing mercy and grace.

To Nick Ciriello—thank you for equipping me with the tools to promote myself as a writer and business owner. Not many authors love marketing, but you've shown me not just how to make it easier but how to create genuinely meaningful conversations around my work.

To my clients at Inkling Creative Strategies—thank you for your patience, flexibility, and encouragement throughout the process of publishing this book. We really are all in this together.

Thank you to Mark Brazaitis, my mentor from the Master of Fine Arts in Creative Writing program at West Virginia University. When you saw something in me, my entire trajectory as a writer changed. Thank you for your ongoing support and friendship.

To Kora Sadler, who devoted her life to encouraging writers in the Akron, Ohio, area, thank you for showing me how essential community is for authors. Your kindness and friendship helped me bridge the awkward gap between my MFA program and life afterward.

Leslie Bustard—you were the first person who told me that the handful of short essays I'd generated by February 2022 could potentially be a book. I have keenly felt your absence throughout this process and am so thankful to have known you.

Thank you to Elaine Reynolds and Becky Thomas for your sparkle as some of the first creative role models I had as a child. The world is more beautiful for you having been in it.

Mom and Dad—thank you for raising me to love the arts. I am thankful for storytelling, Broadway musicals, trips to Disney World, movie nights, and daddy/daughter dates at Borders. Whether it was music, teaching, visual art, acting, or writing, you modeled for me what dedication to one's craft looks like. Because of you, I knew creativity was a special gift long before I discovered that it comes from God.

To my husband, Curtis—I know being married to a writer has been out of your comfort zone and probably not what you expected. Yet, you daily rise to the occasion with grace and sacrifice. Thank you for reading multiple versions of these essays, helping me solve problems, bringing your logical, structured mind to my often unhinged process, helping me deal with frustration, holding down the fort and watching the dog when I went to writing conferences, and of course, driving thirteen hours with me to Georgia to see Flannery O'Connor's house. You make everything I do possible in so many ways. I love you.

Last, all glory, praise, and honor are due to the Lord Jesus Christ, in whom I have redemption through his blood, the forgiveness of sins, according to the riches of his grace. Thank you for using my feeble efforts to do exceedingly abundantly more than I could ask or imagine.

ABOUT THE AUTHOR

Kori Morgan is an author, disciple, and creative entrepreneur from Northeast Ohio. A graduate of Ohio Northern University and West Virginia University's Master of Fine Arts program in creative writing, she has been featured in publications such as *Shenandoah*, *SN Review*, *Blanket Sea*, *Agape Review*, *Switchback*, *Rubbertop Review*, *Solid Food Press*, *Cantos*, and *Clayjar Review*.

Her novel, *The Goodbye-Love Generation*, centers on members of a rock band from her hometown of Kent, Ohio, whose careers are impacted by the shootings at Kent State University in May 1970.

Kori is the founder and Chief Literary Strategist of Inkling Creative Strategies, an author services company that helps writers reach their full creative potential so they can impact and inspire readers. She empowers authors to accomplish this through mentorship, editing, typesetting, and other services at all stages of the writing process.

When she isn't writing or helping authors, Kori enjoys cycling, musical theater, basset hounds, monster truck shows, and vinyl records. She has been married to her husband, Curtis, a machinist and craftsman, since 2011.

Connect with Kori here:
www.korifraziermorgan.com
www.inklingcreative.work
www.instagram.com/writerkori
www.instagram.com/inklingcreativestrategies
www.amazon.com/Kori-Frazier-Morgan/e/B088KTXZMQ/
https://www.facebook.com/korifraziermorgan/